Letters to Juliet:
Is There Life After Death?

A Series of Letters Given Through
Telepathic Correspondence to

JULIET GOODENOW

by the late

Frederic William Henry Myers
Eminent English Author
Scholar and Scientist

ISBN 978-1623390075

Plus the Ink™
An imprint of Minus the Ink™ Digital Publishing Group LLC

FOREWARD

JULIET ELLIS-BEHNKE

My great-grandmother, Juliet Goodenow, and her younger sister, known best as Grace Duffie Boylan, shared a psychic gift: they both were able to telepathically receive messages from people who were dead.

At the turn of the 20th century there was a growing interest in psychic phenomena, led by Frederic Myers, a Cambridge, England classic scholar and writer. He was heavily involved in the investigation of the afterlife and subsequently co-founded the British Society for Psychical Research. Myers speculated that there was a deep region of the unconscious, the "subliminal self," which could account for paranormal events and coined the term "telepathy," derived from the Greek terms tele (distant) and pathe (occurrence or feeling).

Psychic writer Colin Wilson pronounced Myers' 'cross-correspondences', a series of messages from the other side to different mediums in different parts of the world, to be "the most persuasive evidence for the existence for the afterlife." On their own they would mean nothing, but when put together they would make sense. Juliet Goodenow was one of those mediums and in this book, *Letters to Juliet* (originally published under the title *Vanishing Night*), she transcribes the messages telepathically relayed to her by Frederic Myers.

Interest in telepathy increased following World War I as thousands of the bereaved turned toward Spiritualism attempting to communicate with their dead loved ones, evidenced by the multiple printings of her sister's book, *Thy Son Liveth: Messages from a Soldier to his Mother,* after the war. Like the experience of her older sister, Grace Duffie Boylan also received telepathic messages, but these messages were from her son, soon after dying on a battlefield in France. Long out of print, I recently republished *Thy Son Liveth* and it continues to be a top seller, providing comfort to those grieving the loss of loved ones.

Myers invites "a few of my friends" to participate: William Ewart Gladstone, William Shakespeare, Patrick Henry, Ralph Waldo Emerson, William Ellery Channing, Henry Ward Beecher, Disraeli, Abraham Lincoln, George Washington and William James. He invites them to discuss world matters and to relay the information from each person "present at the meeting" into the conscious mind of Mrs. Goodenow. Myers then asks her to explain how she is able to differentiate between the speakers.

TABLE OF CONTENTS

FOREWARD...i

INTRODUCTION...vii

PREFACE...xiii

PART I LAWS OF BEING...1

CHAPTER 1 TRANSCENDENT REALITIES...1

CHAPTER 2   ATTAINMENT OF BEING...5

CHAPTER 3   THE STRATA OF BEING...11

CHAPTER 4   THE CYCLE OF BEING...17

CHAPTER 5   THE UNIT OF LIFE...21

CHAPTER 6   THE GREAT CHANGE...25

CHAPTER 7   WHAT I FOUND TO DO...29

PART II   THE TEST OF PERSONALITY PROOF OF IMMORTALITY...33

CHAPTER 8   THE WONDERFUL PEACE...33

CHAPTER 9   THE WAR PANORAMA...37

CHAPTER 10   JOURNEY THROUGH THE TENUOUS ATMOSPHERE—THE TENDER SHEPHERD...43

CHAPTER 11 MESSAGE TO THE
MOTHERS…51

CHAPTER 12 THE MINISTRY OF HEAVEN:
OCCUPATION, ETC....55

CHAPTER 13 THE PLANETARY
BALANCE…59

CHAPTER 14 THE SHINING LIGHTS OF
HEAVEN…63

CHAPTER 15 MULTIPLE MIND—THE BIRTH
OF AN IDEA…67

CHAPTER 16 THE ELEMENTAL
DISASTER…71

CHAPTER 17 IF A MAN DIES SHALL HE
LIVE AGAIN?...77

CHAPTER 18 THE FAMILY UNIT…81

CHAPTER 19 THE NEW ERA OF PSYCHICAL
RESEARCH…83

CHAPTER 20 THE MASTER CREATION: THE
PROMISE…87

CHAPTER 21 MEMORIES OF CHILDHOOD:
COMPANIONSHIP…93

CHAPTER 22 THE RELATIONSHIP OF GOD
TO MAN…97

CHAPTER 23 LOVE…103

CHAPTER 24   MARRIAGE...107

CHAPTER 25   HEAVEN...111

CHAPTER 26   THE DRAMA OF WORLDS...117

CHAPTER 27   RALPH WALDO

EMERSON...125

CHAPTER 28   LETTER FROM THE

AUTHOR...129

AFTERWORD...131

ABOUT JULIET GOODENOW...134

INTRODUCTION

JULIET GOODENOW

SAN DIEGO, CALIF.
February 15, 1915

Life is religion and science. The two are sisters in one thought and purpose. The creation of Life is scientific; the unfolding of Life is religion. To the enfolded flower within the bud, science at work creates form, color, texture, measurement and estimates power of resistance to sun, rain, wind and climatic conditions.

Geometrically poised on tree or bush, each leaf has the same scientific appointment. When the calyx is unfolded and breathes in the air, religion becomes the Life of the flower. The purity and sweet odor of the flower give back to earth a quickening process of reproduction, which inspires the heart of man to adoration.

To all verdure, to sky, clouds, to mountains, sea and rivers, to grass, plain and valley, is given the interpretation of the soul's cry for the Unknown.

The mystery of Creation speaks to the soul in translation capable of intelligent analysis.

During the closing months of 1912 and during January, 1913, the writer, while in Boston, sent out the first note of inquiry to the Author concerning the human personality. The immediate response is given in this foreword, together with the only other communication received while in Boston. The next correspondence came in California in 1915 when the Author urged the beginning of this notable work. During the year 1916 the work was necessarily delayed, to be resumed in New York City in January, 1917. These letters are presented to the publishers verbatim, together with the original manuscript.

Some time prior to my winter in Boston, I had determined to give up inspirational writing as I had at times obtained that which proved to be error.

A dear one said: "Call someone of a visiting scientific mind. Do you think of one in the higher sphere?" I recalled a book I had read some ten or fifteen years before by Mr. Myers, entitled: "The Survival of Bodily Death."
I remember that the work was analytical and that the author had been called from earth.

Suddenly his name came to my mind. This is all that I knew concerning Mr. Myers. With pen in hand, my sister by my side, I called with my inner voice: "Mr. Myers!" The reply came instantly, as follows:

FIRST LETTER RECEIVED IN BOSTON IN 1912

I am he. It does not take long for a spirit to travel. The first faint allusion to a spirit is heard. The time is advancing when the world shall know more about the world immortal. It is just that it should know. Why you have kept in the background, I cannot imagine, unless you are under Divine command. Undoubtedly you are. You seem to understand why, and surely it is not for me to say you should give up your knowledge. But I am interested that the world should know that open communication may be had with this side at any time, and under conditions strictly normal.

Can you not arrange to write a suitable magazine article on the subject, allowing me to dictate? Your memory has been somewhat injured by the many duties forcing the gray matter of the brain out of the channels of thought into those of action. But you have cells enough to enable you to assimilate a great amount of knowledge. You ask if it will be possible to fill these cells with knowledge after the survival of bodily death. Surely you do not expect to leave these cells of yours behind when you come here! They will expand many times, and concepts will envelope them and introduce a stimulus that will cause your memory to become fixed and natural to your ability—a compensation which is truly appreciated by myself. The main ambition of my heart is to enlighten the world on this one point—that *bona fide* communication with the Unseen Universe is absolute proof of immortality. I am sure of this; but to convince the world requires indubitable proof, which you are able to furnish.

Sincerely yours in the interests of Science.

FREDERIC W. H. MYERS

Boston, Mass., January, 1913

I am most happy to supply any information you may desire and I sincerely wish you would avail yourself of any knowledge I may have, and you know, from my standpoint, I may vouchsafe knowledge as substantially true and authentic without the display of the least egotism. There are many reasons why one could be misunderstood from this source of knowledge. First, the mind is complex—how much so, very few people ordinarily comprehend. There are as many strata of mind as there are sands in the sea or stars in the sky; some of these strata are attuned to lower orders of being and vibrate to thoughts of those within the range of the subconscious mind attuned to receive such vibrations. That this substratum could exist in the same personality seems improbable, but it is true. The higher order of being brings the substrata to higher levels and the lower strata are finally brought beyond the reach of minds out of harmony with the Higher Mind. When at last the personality becomes disenthralled from the lower creation of being, there is less aptitude of deception. True, the mind may wander, or thought may not maintain its equilibrium. Mind is like a bird on the wing: it may soar into the heights and partake of the glory of the gods, or it may descend into the very depths and drink abysmal myrrh. So it is that a medium of expression cannot always be maintained.

I recognize in you a power for good and for untold happiness. Let me come often for the sake of the humanities that are submerged and for the sake of the extension of God's Kingdom.

FREDERIC W. H. MYERS

PREFACE

FREDERIC W. H. MYERS

OCEAN PARK, CALIFORNIA
January, 1915

To the majority of readers, I am aware that an introduction of this nature must be exceedingly difficult to read and somewhat dry. However, it seems quite necessary in a work of this kind where the writer or dictator is in the dark, or in a way invisible to the inquirer; people will naturally inquire into the nature of this correspondence so readily given before the world is quite ready to accept it as genuine, or as authentic.

It is the history of all progress. Growth must be silent until perfection is attained; before the perfect fruit or flower is ripe. Thus we have been advancing in science. The last few years have brought much to light in science and invention; many secrets of nature are rapidly unfolding. The wireless telegraph is analogous to telepathy—for telepathy is the sole process used in the conveyance of these letters from the Here of Life, from the Transcendent to the Vale of Tears. Very few people today repudiate the science of telepathy. The world is rapidly advancing. When this idea is grasped in its entirety, the mystery of communion, prayer and the Voice of God (which voice is the still small voice within the soul of man), will have entered into the conception of man and will be acknowledged as practical as well as scientific.

There is no abnormality in telepathy. There is nothing new in wireless messages, atomically vibrating through space, save in the discovery of the laws governing etheric vibrations. Certain instruments are attuned to vibrations—others are not attuned. All, however, may be attuned under proper conditions. To man, the attunement is inherent in his Being. This is the silken thread which binds soul to soul. This is the call center, the S.O.S. at sea! This is his certain help in time of disaster. There is nothing new in telepathy; it is part of the human personality; severing the soul from the body by death does not rob the soul of culture. The soul contains all that it gained of education and refinement while in the body, advancing in progress.

The mother thinks of her departed child; the child responds, calling, "Mother!" Telepathy reunites them. The child knows mother, but the mother does not know of that power within her being that lies dormant, awaiting development. The brain cells of the average man or woman are capable of very much more development than is generally known. Thought added each day, studying something beyond the generalities, will gradually open unused brain-cell capacity. All may not attain at once; a college course takes years of application. Materiality often obstructs spiritual advancement.

My correspondent is not clairvoyant, neither does she study spiritism, nor attend seances. She is normally attuned to etheric vibrations and is able, through the adaptation of her personality, to synchronize thoughts, imprinted on the retina of her conscious mind. At the same time, her brain causes her hand to transcribe them on paper. This also is a scientific demonstration of a law applying to the human personality, applicable to those who may be willing to qualify.

To understand Truth, we must not only grasp one side of the subject, but all sides, including the inside or the part usually considered immaterial to the end in view. I do not intend entering into any problematical discussion. Rather, it will be my aim to present my views in a simple manner which must of necessity begin with the reader, leading him step by step to the natural and, therefore, logical conclusion concerning the important matter of Life hereafter.

It should be kept in mind that the one who is dictating this paper has passed through the change called Death. That he is today alive, having taken his life, his mentality, his education, his power to reason, his outlook on affairs, into the world beyond the sight of those left behind. I hope to convince you that what is called Death is only the other side of Life. Both sides are necessary to the completed whole of Life's experiences, as two sides are necessary to a structure of any kind. Personally, as I view myself, I am unchanged. I realize now that my garment of flesh was of little importance. We place too great emphasis on material, vanishing substance. This is searching for dew in the warmth of the noonday sun.

I am alive, in the full possession of my five senses, entering into the development of other senses more adaptable to the higher, finer strata of ether. I do not say better—I say *finer,* because attunement is different. Higher, because of unlimited space.

Nature is no charlatan. Most rigid in her demands of exactness, strict to pattern. To humanity she has been lavish in the bestowal of faculties: half she has buried deep within the nature she has so constructed as to conceal her handicraft.

Man could not be great, approaching the Divine counterpart, if faculty could be discerned at a glance, or "man measured as a measure of barley."

The deep recesses of a lofty mountain containing all within and without, are more indicative of man's faculty, his normal self. Life here begins on the Other Side. You do not understand how this can be. The transition moment is the wedge that severs the material from the spiritual.

The spirit bathes in the element it is accustomed to; therefore, the part of us that survives bodily Death, is in its own natural element all of the time. The objective body does not apprehend that Spirit is communing with the great Universal Spirit, obtaining through absorption and vision much that is retained as spiritual culture; when at last the soul breaks away from its envelope of flesh, it is not a stranger in a strange land.

Letters to Juliet

in

Two Parts

———

Part I

Laws of Being

———

Part II

The Test of Personality

Proof of Immortality

PART I LAWS OF BEING

CHAPTER I
TRANSCENDENT REALITIES

January 3, 1915

The subject matter of this book will be facts relating to life on the Sphere commonly known as the hereafter. There is no hereafter; this is a misnomer. All humanity is enveloped in what you call the hereafter, both on this side and the other side of life, as lived in the flesh. To be divested of the body is nothing more than putting aside the worn-out garment for one more worthy of a life on the Higher Sphere. There is no change other than this. Life goes on vibrant, conforming to natural laws, which are the same on both Planes. The worn-out body of flesh is worth the associations connected with it— nothing more, nor less. It clothed the life of an individual that has gone on; the clothing that concealed or contained for a brief period of his existence, was of no more value to him than your last year's suit is to you. Granted this is true, you know that your loved one is gone out of your sight. Here your knowledge ceases, for the poet has written, no traveler has returned to tell of the undiscovered land. We have been left to conjecture, based on human reasoning and belief in divine revelation. I claim that within every organism there is a proof of immortality.

1

Science is unfolding through discovery the intricate powers of Being, from the perfected organism of protoplasm to the perfect man, created in the Image of God. Within this perfect creation is resident a power many fail to find. Nevertheless, it lies deep within the complex nature of mankind. Animals have this power, to some extent. The normal man is a god, but rarely does he come to his estate, through ignorance of his inheritance. It is not so much a matter of choice as it is a matter of development. A man is a bundle of faculties, to use according to his will and education. Some lie so deep within his soul that he fails to discover his treasure of riches. One must become acquainted with one's interior being. There are vast fields of discovery within, worth exceeding scrutiny; there is no wall of division between that interior wall of man on that side and the man free from earth's limitations on this side. To become acquainted with the interior life is to launch a craft on the sea that reaches the shores of Infinity—there is nothing to obstruct your voyage. Your safety lies in your judgment, as sense becomes alert, and capable of analytical experiences. Harmonies reveal the approach of something ideal hitherto beyond the grasp of spiritual sense. You have touched a chord responding to your need; now a harp with a thousand strings plays within your soul. Your inner ear receives the impression of angelic voices; for the veil that separates the seen and the unseen is very thin. You have clasped hands across the border, and interchange of thought and knowledge and correspondence is possible in the exercise of the impression you receive through actual contact with Truth. You should cultivate your impressions, your intuitions—trust them as your guide where you travel and discover by sense. This faculty is easy of cultivation, when the student applies himself to the task. The cultivation of the spiritual will be slow as learning a foreign language; the material must be held in abeyance, or the dross of matter will obscure the transcendent realities awaiting discovery.

Patience??
temporarily suspended
or not used.

London

CHAPTER II
ATTAINMENT OF BEING

OCEAN PARK, CALIFORNIA
January 22, 1915

The rapidity of thought illustrates the flight of spirit; few guess that thought is so rapid in reaching the one to whom thought is given. I may be traveling thousands of miles in some foreign planet unknown to the world, when a thought holds me spellbound and I get the import of it and respond in the same way, my thought attuned to one of my vibrations—by this I mean one who has traveled along the same line of research or one who may be interested in the things I am interested in. To all such, thought is instantaneous. There is absolutely no reason why I should discontinue my journey eastward; if my mission carries me eastward, and a message comes to me from the Pacific Coast, I may address my thought-waves, bidding them attend to receiving all that is attuned to my ear, and likewise I am able to converse with great ease and fluency where there are no cross currents. Let one come who is not in tune, and his magnetic waves cross mine and a ground wire is on—there can be no messages.

Tonight I am riding a white charger with a captain who is marshaling forces—for the world conflict rages here as well as there. The battle-ground of the world lies before us, and were it not for our knowledge of This Side of life, it would seem a most desperate tragedy. We rejoice when every little while one is brought into the light of a perfect day. The world guesses the truth of this onslaught of men—this great, unreasonable war. The warring elements typify other days in history, when the handwriting appeared on the wall. I am not invited to discuss the war, but to invite the attention of the public to the fact of the continuity of life. I wish that I might enter into a logical discussion of the subject in my desire to prove what I know to be a fact. If continuity of life is untrue, then the creation has been a colossal failure; microscopic creation as revealed by strong lenses is perfect in creation, and in the object of creation. All is rhythmic, from the lowest to the intermediate, and on to the highest development of the creature, man. To bring this highest type of creation to the zenith of perfection, and then to destroy him, would be the work of a monster, devoid of intellect or capable of affection or power to continue the creation he has begun.

There is in every nature love of kind. This is deeply imbedded in the lower, as well as the higher types of creation. God, the Creator, has indicated his love for man. The Bible is full of references of God's love for his people—the reasoning is obvious. The most exquisite flower is the violet, almost hid in a mass of protecting leaves. The great secret of the Universe may be revealed to those who carefully brush away doubts, which conceal the truth about important matters lying about, as violets covered with a mass of leaves.

Once again, let me urge you to reason over the truth in your mind—all about you are forces on This

Side of life. You are being bathed in a spiritual ether, as your thought intrudes the Spheres. Think much of this. Spiritual ether is full of vibrant Truth—in time your thought will assimilate Truth, which will become to you an experience beyond dispute. I learned this truth about my inner receptivity while on the Other Side of life. I found on my arrival here that my intuition had not been false to my conviction of Truth.

Many people on the Other Side have reasoned this out, and no other evidence of the continuity of life is necessary.

SAN DIEGO, CALIFORNIA
April 21, 1915

From this letter I shall endeavor to satisfy the craving in the minds of those who long for the revealment of that which the eye has not seen nor the hearing fully revealed—until the fulfillment of vision comes with the going out of the Vital Spark, called the Breath of Life.

The universal opinion has been and is today that life ends with that which has commonly been called death. This is the greatest mistake man has ever made, and because of this belief thousands of millions have gone down to the grave in terror of soul, believing themselves the victims of a relentless fate. If this were true, it would be the cataclysm of human destiny— impossible to the conception of love, contrary to the human or divine tenderness, the love of father for child, the creator for the created in his image.

Life becomes altogether different when divested of the veil of flesh that has always obstructed the vision. This alone closes out the view that is transcendent about us all.

It is my intention to define the life on This Side as clearly as possible, that all dread may be removed from those whose passing may be soon. Fear may be substituted by peace of mind and rest of body in the assurance that life is continuous. The invisible world about us contains much that is beautiful, as well as the reverse. To those who love the beautiful and hate the opposite, there is little to apprehend or to fear. Mind attracts like mind, and we draw to us those whom we wish. In my garden the flowers I love bloom and birds sing—the same birds that flutter about your gardens—the same butterflies also come into my garden that light on your trellises; the same bees make honey here that contribute to your table the sweets of the hive; the same grass that you have in your lawns—and the trees abound. There is nothing unnatural here. Little toads hop along my path; and frogs leap and bound here in the pools about the garden—grasshoppers fly about and daddy-long-legs attract little children as they did when I was a boy and chased them to get my direction.

The possibility of enlarging the horizon of our spiritual vision is very great. The masses of the people fail to obtain the necessary requirements in this busy life so full of the needs of the body.

Concentration of thought alone prepares the mind to receive impressions. It is of infinite importance that I give you some idea of the importance of searching after Truth. Do not begin the search aimlessly; expect to find what you are looking after—if it is the analysis of a problem that is within the range of your analytical power of comprehension, you will find the answer. If you are searching after melody, the harp of a thousand strings will vibrate the chords of desire. To know this is power!

This lies within the boundary of every life—not only those gifted intellectually, but the world's middle or lower classes may enrich their vocabulary and vision. The quiet hour, interpenetration, expansion and propelling the fixed idea, holding it firm within the mind until the brain power behind it views it from all directions and becomes acquainted with the new product that leads on to other and greater ideas, still on and still further on until illumination of the mind reveals Truth in all her charm and loveliness.

CHAPTER III
THE STRATA OF BEING

February, 1915

The stratum of being is the fundamental truth of life advancing with the development of species from birth to the transition of life on This Side, rounding out the period to continue evolution. To the babe whose full life is rounded out on the higher plane, the advancement is made rapidly, as errors of belief and unscientific methods of life retard progress; the scholar or scientist who has gained access to universal thought through vibration is lifted by his progress to a higher stratum of thought—through his aspiration, knowledge is attained. The abridgment of soul capacity is optional; "to him that has, shall be given, and from him that has not shall be taken even that which he has." This is an arbitrary fact, a scientific truth worth considering.

Dr. James and I often discuss the matter of imparting to the world knowledge that may be of infallible worth. James thinks that we must rely on the human personality itself, for there is resident in everyone a substantiation of truth. The seeker after truth finds a response to his search identical with the thing he searches after. If after reading my words and the facts I relate, my co-workers feel that the character of the words and subject matter expressed are characteristic of me, I am suggested to the minds of my more intimate friends. We may borrow words *ad infinitum*, but style attaches to the author, as the fit of a suit. There is nothing convincing, but has some relative correspondence somewhere. If I direct your attention to a leaf in my ledger, to the name of a friend who borrowed five hundred francs from me, and ask you to collect the same and return it to the family I left, and in searching the files you find the identical book, you may conclude that this is proof sufficient. But it is really of very little worth to prove conclusively that someone on the Other Side imparted this information.

The fact that so little valuable information has been given in this way should be sufficient to prove not a fraud, but that people do not know that they are unscientific in this. Science should discover a way of definite understanding of Truth. If I am able to direct the attention of my co-workers to a line in my ledger, when I should be directing my God-given power and the privilege of communicating with them, to acquaint the public with something of value, why should a life transcending the border come back to speak of trivial things? Dr. James suggests that seekers after truth may depend on interior deduction or inference, proving the truth by experiment; if the experimentation proves to be correct, the same may be depended on, as the same law applies here as there, applicable on both sides of life.

There are teachers here who are glad to communicate knowledge. The way of understanding is the way to knowledge. Many men here are scientifically advanced, far beyond the horizon of my vision. I may not be able to explain simply, as faculty enlarges the understanding; I am not able to ascertain how far the understanding has advanced since my coming here. It is not that men do not know, but not having been far enough on a journey, the horizon shuts in the view—be this as it may, I am constantly learning something. There is no more interesting study to me than the human personality. I have said what every thinking man knows: that Nature is harmonious; that man and stars are the same product. The thought I have in mind is that of Strata of Being, delicate, too refined, too intricate for discussion. We seem to be on Holy Ground. The Creator has covered this subject with a veil that is now to be lifted for the understanding of all the world. Strata of Being, sacred words, expressive of more than you may imagine, with all the imagination of the intellect. Had I the gift of language—but here language is expressed in countless million ways. The voice is but a feeble instrument—words are so many toys of speech. The Strata of Being, the mind at once associates strata with rocks, or mountains, or earth formations; for life is mosaic, built of gem thoughts, here and there a jewel of intrinsic value, here a thorn or briar—a rose or stubble, life values incorporated in Being.

Who has been given choice of what he finds within his being? There is resident in the human personality so many Strata of Being, that any one of these strata might contain a minimum of knowledge equal to any I might seek to impart. Be this as it may, I must write in the language men are wont to speculate in.

The creation of man is the height of creative power, as one half the creative power is portrayed on that side of life. It is impossible to gain a dear idea of what man's nature contains or its tremendous possibilities. To understand this is difficult of comprehension, even after the Change, unless much time is given to studying the subject. My study while there gave me hope to continue; to some extent, I have been able to gratify my ambition.

Man makes selection of what he finds; he chooses his values. His garden is Self—undivided, invisible, interior self. For the interior Self, or Being, is all that is worth discussing—or all that man has to deal with in the last analysis. I use this guardedly: to some it may convey a thought of definite judgment—but the expression is valueless—it is rhetorically fine, but of no significance, as there never will be the last analysis. Had I been given the power to behold my Being, as I view it now, I would have gathered together more of the best there was given for my selection.

Today I am given the opportunity of lighting a candle and placing it on a high hill, that it may shine into many lives. Where did this conglomerate come from that found entrance into the life of man? From the same source that vital energy comes from and hurls planets through space! This is not figurative language, and only one of a million of sources the most remote ancestor has given of ages beyond him. The brain staggers! Nature's contribution of all her attributes is fathomless. Within this creation are faculties unused within the span of life there; occasionally one reaches out into infinitude and discovers harmonies; one makes a chart—again other harmonies and new and vastly different experiences. He is reaching different Strata of

Being and learning the way into the Holy of Holies of life. He feels now the vibration that unites the seen with the unseen. This is not attained by magic. It is the natural growth of the within—or spiritual being. All are created with the same ability of proving the accuracy of this statement. This is the "straight and narrow way" of scriptural utterance, because of its difficult attainment.

CHAPTER IV
THE CYCLE OF BEING

SAN DIEGO, CALIFORNIA
April 13, 1915.

The information I am prepared to give is valuable to the world as coming from one who made a study of psychical research while on the nether side of life. This is helpful to me for information gained from education along any line of thought, whatsoever it may be, is helpful to the student on this side of life.

We know by the very nature of things that mind touches mind—be it on this side or the other. The infringement of thought is one of the most frequent sources of irritation we have to contend with—not knowing our interior self, we cannot account for the interference, and often feel baffled and unable to understand why we are disturbed and unable to think collectively.

The minute fiber of the brain offers little resistance to impressions. While this is valuable beyond language to portray, the ether in which the human is submerged, is electrically charged—some magnets more highly charged, giving out a greater dynamic force, attract similar magnets in different bodies; to the instructed in physics, this will be clear enough. However, we are laboring in the dark. To feel obstructions we cannot see arouses fear and resistance.

This very resistance is contrary to the result we might hope for, could we see the interior life as it is. Open all the avenues of approach. Whatever comes to you is gain—this is product of your own building, the result of your desire, the training you have received, your implement of research and the longed-for missing link of discovery. This is achievement. The inventor— the man of genius—the poet, recognizes that education is fundamental to knowledge. That which the mind receives during the years of education becomes the nucleus, the negative or impression-wax of all that comes along the years of active experience in placing in adjustment theories we have believed to be true.

We are constantly finding out that knowledge, through experience, is overthrowing ideas that once were taught in the universities. That nations fall through the error of man-made conception of principle. Germany is suffering today, in consequence of her having accepted as truth the writings of misguided theorists, involving the world in a conflict of opinion. Materialists have accomplished this tragic result through the materialistic belief of the nation. Education has been Germany's strong bulwark before all nations of the world today.

The student understands that education, as taught by this nation through the wisdom of her universities, has changed her day into night.

Nations that overdevelop materialistic ideas lose the necessary spiritual balance to retain sufficient equilibrium. I deviate somewhat from my subject, to prove the essential things we should endeavor to obtain—

knowledge throws upon experience a searchlight. We have learned that within is the universal way leading to this Wisdom.

It is not so much what you will find when you come to this side of life as what you will bring with you.

April 24, 1915

Sleep is the best definition of death I know anything about—just going to sleep unafraid, to awake in a new and beautiful room, and to be satisfied. This is all there is. About us are our dear friends and loved ones, our children coming on before we have been invited to come. It is the glad coming-home to rest, after a toilsome journey; there are no more anxious days or nights; the changes here are atmospheric—natural, wholesome. A world, within a world, of different appointments, scientifically opposite. The Upper World is the world I am in, living on the Other Side of life. I am rounding out the cycle of my life begun there on the Lower Side— the other side or the Lower Side is as essential as the Upper Side, that which I have entered.

The system is one with many systems, governing the Universe. The only mystery is that of silence concerning this higher development, understanding of which belongs to this sphere of progress and concerning which the concepts of man's brain is mute. To man is given brain cells for the cycle of Being. That all these tissues are not developed on the Lower Side of life, is evidence of another phase of existence that will call into activity tissues prepared for a finer susceptibility, a broader understanding.

April 25, 1915

Human life together with life, all is life, speaking with accuracy; all is organization and has its orbit. This is a figure of speech to illustrate motion—for all life is motion. The form of life we are holding up to analysis is the human element; I repeat the word, organization, as this word illustrates more fully my meaning. From the embryonic state to the end of the first stage, life continues to operate its various functions independent of any means other than contributory elements in which life is submerged—air being the chief element. All Nature contributes to sustain life from the human to the vegetable and mineral, cradled in immensity, suckled at the breast of nature, it survives all disintegrating substances out of harmony with its supply.

CHAPTER V
THE UNIT OF LIFE

OCEAN PARK, CALIFORNIA
February 2, 1915

The condition of the world today is peculiarly adaptable to spiritual investigation. Changes are going on atmospherically, inducing a magnetic influence, attracting the mind to spiritual forces. The open mind may gain access to truth through the continuous vibration going on in the elements. This of itself is a valuable source of information—none need complain of lack of education in spiritual matters. The world is an open book full of vast research. The applied spiritual power may control this information, as lightning is controlled, and when once the application is tested, there is no limit to the universal understanding of all mysteries.

The only way Truth may be obtained, is through the culture of experience; I may describe the beauties of nature in which I have my spiritual being and my spiritual home, I may tell you radiant stories of my surroundings, but this will only interest the curious and edify those who seek amusement. My purpose is to explain a way that may lead to a discovery of your own powers of investigation, disclosing what to you will be a vision surpassing anything previously imagined. To those unacquainted with spiritual traveling, may I suggest that conscience is a good route to begin with. Many endeavor to evade or quiet the conscience, having been taught that it is the voice of God, condemning certain acts or conduct and only used to admonish or to punish the offender—as we dread scolding, so have we dreaded the voice of conscience; to be sure conscience mirrors truth and is a direct way of understanding—it is the gate leading within and beyond the boundaries usually traveled by those on the Other Side of life.

There is no reason why the soul of man should not look on life as a unit. It is his prerogative as a divine being. To accomplish this needs preparation, as any accomplishment or art needs preparation or certain culture. This is not religion, as commonly believed on the Other Side; life rounded out as view on This Side of life is nothing but religion; science is religion; all converges to the point of cleavage when soul is supposed to separate from body—one remains, the other disappears. The religious part is supposed to disappear; now, as a matter of fact, both disappear—you know that one disintegrates, and after that you are as much in the dark as before. Here we usually stop thinking much about the matter, leaving it for Eternity to explain; this question you can circumnavigate.

Science exposes the cerebral cavity as unexplored to even half its brain cells. What the other half holds in reserve for our enlightenment, we are free to admit we do not know. Our containers are empty, while we go about trying to find out from someone else what Nature has endowed us with, with marvelous generosity; nor is this difficult of attainment. To find a gold mine is difficult, because of our ignorance of the stratum of earth, but the Strata of Being contain the Unit of Life.

CHAPTER VI
THE GREAT CHANGE

January, 1915

The astral body contains the embryonic cellular sphere that dissolution of the material does not destroy. This contains in reverse form the concepts of the brain cells used during the life on earth. Here there is the added multiform with its tissues, containing much more than has been received by the brain, but sufficiently strong to make impressions. These faint impressions are preserved, and when introduced into the light on this side, become legible and distinct. The individual recalls the faint impression and the memory adds to its receptive powers *ad infinitum,* others, etc.

Thus you will see that we do not come into a strange life or atmosphere. That which comes is habituated, and naturally continues to live and move and have its being in its natural environment, its home element.

Physical lungs, heart and body being material, would be stranger to this side, as they belong only to the initiatory state of being. That which does belong and is native to this element finds no difficulty or strangeness here. All is natural and homelike about the soul released and able to swing free, and continuing to remain free.

There is no sorrow here. The joy of release is very great, as one ushered out of prison into a new and beautiful country. Here atmospheric conditions enhance beauty and colors; the perfume of flowers sweeter than those of earth and more perfect in form and color, having passed the rudimentary stage, as expressed in the initial period.

When first I came, I did not comprehend that a change had taken place. I had become somewhat familiar with the place I found myself in, nothing seemed unnatural—when suddenly I became aware that my cloak was gone. I reached out my hand, thinking it had fallen on the ground. I observed there was no ground under my feet. I found myself in the air, slightly moving. A friend was near me. He spoke casually of a new specimen he had found. I was greatly surprised at my discovery, and very much elated that I had passed the Great Ordeal. I wanted then to return and tell the world the truth of life and the wonders of the Transition to this Side.

I spoke to my friend, interested in his new specimen. He told me that I appeared so unconcerned about my new life that he had watched to see what I would do when at last I discovered myself. My mind instantly reverted to those loved ones left behind. I wondered if they knew I had departed on my Long Journey. I wanted so much to take my long farewell and to tell them how much I loved them and how eagerly I should await their coming. This condition of mind drew me nearer to earth, where I could feel the sorrow of my family and friends. Here I stayed, feeling helpless to leave, sorrowing for those whom I had left so abruptly. Many others were also close to the earth, within the magnetic circle of earthly joys and human affection. Suddenly I felt the desire to lift their thoughts with mine to the life I had entered so quietly; I felt my life drawing them—I had lifted them into a different sphere of thought where they received comforting assurances; we seemed to meet on the old familiar plane. I know they felt my presence, as I did theirs.

Then I came into the upper atmosphere, to begin my life work, endeavoring not to allow distraction to deter me from my pursuit of knowledge.

I desired to find my home. A guide appeared on the way, and I followed him. We traveled what seemed a long distance. I marveled that I was so far from home. Distances do not seem to be so great. I knew that I had seen my home before—it seemed very natural. Here I found several of my favorite books—a friend had placed them there. Shortly after my home-coming, a number came in for a friendly chat; nothing seemed strange or unnatural here. The strange or unnatural seemed not to belong here, but to that other side where, beginning as a babe, I had rounded out my earthly existence.

CHAPTER VII
WHAT I FOUND TO DO

SAN DIEGO, CALIFORNIA
May 11, 1915

I had not been here long before I realized my opportunity of service, which is always waiting response in the soul. I discovered many on this side wandering about untaught, spiritually, who had, many of them, made a success in material things, but of the inner life that prevails here, were ignorant. One man whom I knew in New York recognized me as I passed his home in one of the lesser streets, for streets and avenues here are not unlike those below. We find our station in life here, as there, and find our homes according to our wealth; but the coin of exchange is not barter in the market places, as you anticipate. It is measured by what a man has gained of spiritual worth, it may be that riches have been his in material things as well as spiritual. This does not mean so much the spiritual knowledge or education he may have received in his college course or academic training— but it means self-sacrifice for others, for the sake of others—not for earthly gain—but for the love of others, preferably to self. One who ministers to his own life for the sake of self, exhausts spiritual growth and dwarfs his life, closing the curtains, admitting no rays of light from without, and finally exhausting his own supply of light thereby, living in darkness and returning to the same element when he passes to the other side of life. To these people dwelling in darkness, we often go. They love to welcome us for the shining light of those of us who have been able to gain admittance to the light by means of what may be a different environment, or a right starting point, is most brilliant.

These poor souls are anxious to begin their study, as the physical and the material is all they have. The spirit came naked and starved. Ministering angels are always about them, giving themselves to the work of instruction and leading them into the light of assimilation. This flood-tide bathes them in ether and impressions, as a child in school studies the blackboard.

The homes of these people, dwelling in darkness, are quite bare and devoid of ornamentation. Please understand this is not arbitrary. They have made a choice and must abide by the selection of life they have chosen. Man, being a free agent, cannot be coerced into changing his life except by his own free will.

May 16, 1915, 5:30 P.M., Cloudy

This afternoon, a company of men and women attended the exposition, examining with much pleasure the architecture and general arrangement of the grounds. "Science of Man" attracted me, of course, and I have been exceedingly gratified to see the interest people are taking in this important feature of the work.

The day is peculiarly adapted to the atmospheric needs of the released spirit—the withdrawal of the sun's rays and the adjustment of electrical vibrations.

QUESTION:
Do the electrical vibrations interfere with the spirit in any way?

ANSWER:
You wish to inquire if we are troubled by the influx of electricity in our nearing the Earth?

The electrical fluid permeates the atmosphere at great heights, and we are familiar with its contact. It in no manner affects the spirit robed in vapor, other than to make more luminous our appearance—light, however, is different, absorbing our veils completely in diffusing thought. This explains why communication is difficult when the sun shines. On cloudy days, hosts of shining ones visit the earth and mingle with friends and loved ones. These days are significant for rejoicing here, and much gain is received by the earth in consequence. We convey, to those whom we visit, spiritual blessings. What we believe—the thoughts we bear our friends— are enriched by contact with their thought. This is communion, often unrecognized, save by a sense of exaltation—a feeling of content, a sense of well-being.

May 17, 1915, 12 M

The importance of clearly finding the relationship between the seen and the unseen is exceedingly great. The only barrier to this law governing both worlds is that of mortal sight. This is physical, and therefore not permanent. The emphasis on this word *physical* makes my meaning clear.

Life is spiritual and touched on all sides by the spiritual universe; interpretation through the sense, independent of the physical eyesight, may be obtained by the cultivation of the Inner Life, as already explained in these pages. All *is* natural. There is nothing abnormal in creation, as God created the universe in harmony, subject to certain irrevocable laws, transgression of which introduces the only abnormality we know anything about.

As seasons come and go in the round of climatic changes, so Life revolves on its axis and departs after having performed its function for which it found expression on the lower plane. All is natural and government is radical; being prearranged at the time life and worlds began as a system. I cannot explore the life I live here, on this side of life, without first bringing the mind into subjection of there being but one life, and the continuity of it extending into Infinitude.

PART II
THE TEST OF PERSONALITY
PROOF OF IMMORTALITY

CHAPTER VIII
THE WONDERFUL PEACE

NEW YORK CITY
January 11, 1917

There are many gathered here in this cozy home this evening, and much importance is attached to this renewal of the work begun so long ago in California. Times are changing there, and we are concerned that the world should learn more of the facts as they are—so much is written of bloodshed and battles and wrongs committed; of woe and desolation, that we have thought best to lift the thought of the world into the atmosphere higher up, where there is peace and where there is no thought of inharmony and war.

The world knows its sorrow, and now, as never before in its long and faithful history, the people of the world are surfeited with the horror of war in its dire details. Let us forget war in our future discussion, and leave the world of the flesh and the limitations of the body and ascend into this realm of the Universe where peace is everlasting and eternal.

This is not theoretical, it is scientific, and will readily be accepted as such as we proceed to explore the vistas of the stars. The humanities are engaged in binding up bruises, but these are bruises of the soul and of the spirit that we are able to bind up and enrich with the wisdom of the universe. "Come unto me, all ye that labor and are heavy-laden and I will give ye rest"— Jesus taught Science more than he taught Religion. This scientific statement is the outcome of the heart's impulse to reach out to that which will satisfy the need of the soul. The body reclines on a smooth surface and may be rested and refreshed—not so the soul; the man himself is urged by his restlessness to the verge of despair— where, oh where, can he find rest and quiet of spirit? His soul is aflame with the tragedy of life, the mockery of existence. One speaks! Commanded by Omnipotence—out of the void comes answer to the need of the soul. *Come unto me. Free as a bird.* All this is figurative language and is suggestive of a place of peace; not a dogmatic utterance, but the essential need of one who was born of woman and acquainted with grief.

Here there is the shield and the buckler, the defender of the race, and the invitation circles the universe of souls.

To be lifted up above the web of fate that encircles a man like a chain, binding him to conditions impossible of change, is the work of the Master Builder, the Creator of man and of the world and systems of worlds. Man is the master of his fate—the creator of his destiny. The invitation is expressed in kingly language and to the inheritors of kingdoms. To men on the earth plane by One who had lived the earth life and knew the sorrows of the soul, and who had in his wisdom discovered the remedy of relief. There is peace, wonderful peace very near—and to those who do not know of this by experience, let me suggest a way to find it.

I am writing to men and women of grown stature, students of art and of literature, physics and invention, etc. You will not find it in books—the wisdom of children is considered to be worth more than the wisdom of sages. The 'within' of the soul. The intellect of the interior being instructs; books often imitate and reflect, distorting images as shadows in some stagnant pool.

January 12, 1917

Tonight the hosts about us are full of the thoughts of helpfulness to the world as never before; the windows of heaven are open to the cry of those who suffer, and ministering spirits are busy with the cry of those who yearn for peace and for solitude in the stress of disaster. The most appalling disaster of time nearing eternity. All here are laboring to bring about a righteous peace. There is no time to waste. We are onlookers of a terrible holocaust; we look away, to return to our labors with a feeling of intense desire to work longer and to accomplish greater results.

The thought of the world suffering in the throes of war that shows no sign of abatement, the spread of hate and of revenge, the spirit of greed, the distress of nations unparalleled in the world's history, is the torch that sets all heaven ablaze with sympathy!

CHAPTER IX
THE WAR PANORAMA

January 19, 1917

I look out over the world tonight, I see much that is sorrowful there on the Earth Plane. But those of us who see both sides are glad to read the story of it all as we see it—Here. Those children of sorrow below are beginning their earlier entrance to life Here; and millions who might have extended sorrowful lives of hardship and penury, are now in the fields of bounty, and in the enrichment of culture, and beginning the study of whatever they most desire to learn. There are groups of classes everywhere. The hillsides are full of children and half-grown boys and girls, men and women lately arrived, reveling in their new experience—for never before have there been so many strange people of all nations in heaven at once. Interpreters are about, modifying languages and teaching groups to understand each other. All are deeply concerned with the affairs they have suddenly left, and it is with much precaution that your hand is guarded. Do not fear—you are safe—but you may well imagine how eagerly the veil is scanned that separates us.

One little child running about here is crying for "Mother!" And just now, a sweet woman who had left her little ones, gathered the child to her bosom and said in soft French, *"Oui ma cherie, la mere!"* The little one nestled close and both were wafted away content in finding solace in the companionship of loving need.

A little boy, alone, is wandering about, catching toads, and putting them in a basket—he has a net tied to a stick and holds it where the toads jump into it. He seems to be happy and it is not yet evident to him that his mother is not here. But the Lord watches over His own and the little lambs torn from the fold are given into the care of angels whose life work is the care of the young. And here happiness and growth seem never to fail in masterful sequence—for boys and girls grow strong in appearance and more beautiful in maturity. They are not hardened by speculative pursuits, nor engaged in working out the problems of existence, nor keeping at bay the proverbial wolf—but gather into their faces the sunshine of culture, of things pertaining to growth and development of life here.

Many are interested in musical composition, for here the harmonies are listed and easily attuned to the most delicate vibrations. The most exquisite musical compositions I have ever listened to are played by those whose musical desires have never had the opportunity to expand until coming here. One young miss of fifteen seems to be able to play the harp, although she never owned one below; and the fact that she has a harp makes her very happy, and she plays it pretty much all the time. Nobody tires of listening, for all is culture, and progress is very fast.

One old man sits by the gate leading into a valley where sheep are browsing; he has a jew's-harp and the twang of this jew's-harp is not unlike the sound produced years ago, when I first played one at school.

Well, of this motley assemblage enough has been said. You will wonder where they stay and if homes are provided, and what they are like, and what is the management of such a large community, and all about it.

January 20, 1917

The times are full of interest unparalleled in the world's history. On This Side, we see life as it is; our viewpoint is continuous, as our sense of continuity is undiminished; we have not only that of sight, but of intuition—the feeling that goes with comprehension. The fact that nothing obstructs the vision is a factor coupled with sense that gives freedom to our faculties.

The war panorama that engages our attention is a part of every day and night task, for we are mobilized for work in companies, by tens, by hundreds, by fifties, by thousands; we have complete organizations engaged in active service. Some of our men are trained for military maneuvers; others are learning tactics from those in command. This will seem strange to you, but you will readily see that we are unchanged in the transition of life, and to be severed from our tentacles of flesh does not impair faculties in the least. In fact, they are more alert and ready for whatever there is to do. Before the breaking out of the war, most people were engaged in the discovery of worlds and exploration in science, teaching, traveling and listening to discourses from teachers unparalleled in learning, making observations through specially constructed lenses, analyzing light spectrums, and making studies of chemistry in relation to new scientific discoveries. Botany takes much interest, and the Valley of Art attracts numerous painters who take huge canvases and tack them to trees, and there they sketch for hours. The work accomplished is quite beautiful, as here art is unrestricted and the supply of material both in the concrete and in the abstract is abundant. The mountains stretching about us are veritable symphony centers; sound travels better, and certainly the music heard in the evening is the sweetest imaginable; for here are the singers of all time, who love harmony and who themselves express it. But, to return to the mobilization of armies, and to the thought of war in this place beyond the Vale of Tears. Here we have the universal view-point. Having attained the spirit of immortality, we have let loose the mortal coil and that sense of bitterness that is kin to matter, as rust is to iron.

Whatever may have been our preference before we arrived on the plane of present comprehension, we are able to define motive and hold nations to strict account for violation of the laws of humanity. To Germany belongs the sword that will turn and pierce her side asunder. She has listened to false doctrines and has forgotten the laws governing Being. And the same law governs both nations and the life of individuals which comprise nations. "As ye sow, so shall ye reap," is inevitable in its results. As the sower casts the seed in the field, reaping his reward in season—so with the nation that sows hate, discord, wanton murder and rapine, the inevitable disaster returning to destroy that nation will come on the wings of the whirlwind from heaven, for we are the avengers of men, sent on our mission to heal or to destroy; for "as ye sow, so shall ye reap," is science in the concrete. There is no other way for individuals or for nations. We are the masters of our fate, the creators of our destiny—would that we might bind up the bruises of those who suffer mightily!—but the whirlwind is let loose and the Demon of War must be satisfied until the time of the return of the Avenger.

There is little need for dwelling longer on this subject of war, save to say the time is near for the capitulation. Would that it might be the surrender of bitterness and hatred of the kins-people of Europe! For hatred in the land is breathed and engendered in the life of men and animals, and in food products, creating much distress and famine and contagious disease.

SAN DIEGO, CALIFORNIA
May 17, 1915

This is my preparation for the travel tour we are preparing to make—for my spirit, winged with yours, produces a multiple of spirit and I will give the light I have obtained as we proceed on our journey of observation with no less vigor than I had, but with an added sense of unlimited ability to describe, which my tongue sometimes refused coherently to express, while wearing my coat of flesh.

As I prepare for my journey through ether, I am wearing a luminous garment, floating closely to my form, as I move through space. This garment radiates light from the shining form it veils. This light is mine, and it is the heritage of every created soul, placed there by the Creator of all life, and is the glory of God revealed in the flesh—while in the body, preserved in the soul, lighting the spirit in its search for eternal Truth.

You bring with you the luminous veil, when you come. Some are more beautiful, showing a fine tracery of exquisite design which I am told is the crystallized thoughts of its wearer. Mine is somewhat common compared to many here; I wish that I had known in that day of my preparation that each of my secret thoughts was in the weaver's shuttle and in the day of my advancement would be given to me as the adornment of my spirit, made luminous by the light of my soul, that all might read the history of my preparation. . .

CHAPTER X
JOURNEY THROUGH THE TENUOUS
ATMOSPHERE—THE TENDER
SHEPHERD

NEW YORK CITY
January 28, 1917, 4:30 P. M

Today we shall take a journey together into the nearby regions of space and as we ascend into the ether, I will tell you so far as I am able to, of the things passing my eyes.

We shall imagine that we are being carried along on some vehicle of locomotion; it will be easier for you to imagine that, as the imagination often plays quite a part in the success or failure of any enterprise whatever—even that of an imaginary journey, which in fact is not at all imaginary, from my viewpoint; but from your viewpoint, may be, according to your present limited viewpoint.

I wish I might convey plainly the fact of human personality as it is; for upon this premise I could explain why you are not imagining what seems to be strictly imagination, in the fact that you are quietly writing my thoughts telepathically impressed upon the retina of your eye, as well as upon that of your brain, at the same time synchronizing your nerve muscles which have the ability to transcribe it on paper. At the same moment you are whirling through space, for your thought is you as much as your body is you, and your mind becomes cognizant of all that is passing. This may sound erratic, because such ideas are unfamiliar to most of us unacquainted with the human personality.

Let it be strictly understood that you do not exercise abnormal faculties. It is not in my province as a scientist to instruct the world in the study of esoteric philosophy. The world must revolve some time before atmospheric changes are sufficient to induce such study without disorganization of brain structure, if brought in contact with atmosphere charged with the vapors of an atmosphere suitable to the tenuous forms of life. I do not in any way decry research work or study of secret doctrines, for the enlargement of faculty or for the advancement of science,—but I warn people who try to bring the two atmospheres together for the purpose of investigation for amusement, or for entertainment of those who are curious minded. This is disharmonious and is not intended for those on mortal planes.

It may be accomplished, but I urge scientists not to make investigations along such lines. It is rare that one on This Side will enter into negotiation with those whose object; it is to entrap the unwary. But here, as well as there, are those who are curious and anxious to appear to their friends; but those of us who resort to such means are often delayed in our ability to ascend into higher realms of activity.

Psychics do not commonly understand that atmospheric conditions are the only barriers to sight of the Unseen. This is true. Finally, this will gradually change. Within the last few years the tenuity of the air has been changed so as to render the sense of vibration less difficult; with this preamble, we may take our journey into the highly tenuous atmosphere. Let us turn our thoughts as far away from earth as we may, as we ascend into the higher realms of space. While we may observe that other vehicles occasionally are seen, they are not in our own atmosphere. We are enfolded within a higher form of vapor, radiating light and exhilaration to all who are privileged to enjoy it. Only man's thought or spirit could enjoy the privilege—his soul is already resident of this sphere—so you will not feel afraid or un-at-home when you at last venture to come alone.

But now we are traveling fast and as I gather my robe my thought, with yours, is eager to see what there is of interest. Beyond the hedge over there on the hillside, I see a man urging a little boy to follow him. The little one came yesterday—I can tell by his footsteps and by his aimless manner. Now the man is taking him up in his arms, and beyond, over on the Other Side of our tenuous atmosphere, is a woman reaching towards this little child with eager, outstretched arms—with the disappearance of the man and boy, the woman returns to her home, and is quieted. A sense of peace comes into her heart.

The office of the tender shepherd is accomplished. Little children always find a tender shepherd, and mothers yet to follow their little heart-treasures, need not wring their hearts in helplessness, for the Angels watch over them.

You will soon see by observation as we travel on, that distance is not measured as you are accustomed to measure it below. For Here the rapidity of thought is accentuated—we have traveled far. Over there in the hazy distance is Australia, a most wonderful country, with an ideal form of government. Please observe the clearness of the atmosphere overhanging the island empire. The people of this country are peaceful, and the effect of harmony is felt even in the stars over their heads. We are now nearing Europe. Observe the difference. See the streams of gray enveloping the air like clouds of dingy vapor—we hurry past. Up higher, we feel glad that our atmosphere is beyond the sorrow of war and its bitterness.

Let us wait by this wicket gate for a moment, while the battle rages on the Somme. I dislike keeping you here to see the agony of war enacted, but your spirit is able to bind up bruises—and as we wait here, our compassion assuages grief; here is a lad. We are in time to help him.

We are glad to be of service to you—we are friends from home, and we are leading you; on and on they come. Well, this is the beginning of real work. Let me aid you—just keep your balance, while I touch the lad's corsage. He has dropped his sword, never again to use it, praise Heaven! Let us go—we are among so many ascending spirits; we are guiding them and helping them. You are not afraid. Your spirit is helping them with the courage you have acquired in your life of victory. Others are coming for these boys in white—we shall meet them again, for the organization of this world is most perfect; and having met and greeted, we shall see them again.

The sky is ablaze with the lights of suns and stars. We see in passing they are inhabited. Creation is very old. Space is illimitable. Our Earth is a dot in space. You tremble at immensity. Over there in the purple mist is Mars.

You have watched the Red Star from your doorstep. Notice the temples devoted to art, and the volume of sound that issues from the cathedrals.

Many of the Martians are untaught; hewers, of wood and carriers of water still exist wherever life is found.

Those stars in the distance are void of life, having swung out of the life atmosphere. Saturn and Antares are among them. Many caves abound, and some are quaint in jewels—very rare, as we count precious gems.

Over there, by the side of the Euphrates river, was the Garden of Eden—see the little plot of green—where our first parents stumbled for their disobedience. How little we understand the vehicles of speech, and how "blindly we go about, leading the blind."

On our return to our own habitations, yours in a corner of a great city, encircled by tall buildings and walls of stone, within the shelter of four walls and under the radiance of the pink glow of the evening lamp, and I to my mansion in the sky, eternal in the heavens, "that fades not away"; come for a moment and meet my friends gathered here for a visit. The balcony is my den. There, under the violet dome of brass is a collection of gems I have been gathering in my walks. The paths are full of them. Those I have for my dome are really very fine specimens of bellum amethysts.

Most of it was deeply imbedded in rock. This stick in the corner came from Babylon, by the river we passed this afternoon, and contains some hieroglyphic history a friend of mine is able to decipher.

This window overlooking the garden is where I sit while making my charts of exploration, and where I often gather the children for a study in nature. Here is a cobweb of silken mist; there in the corner is the spider—probably has noticed a stranger, and thinks to run. Animals, insects, birds and fishes are not blind to tenuous atmosphere—even this little grasshopper on my rose trellis would take note of an adventurous Ghost from the, Other Side.

This is the mint of my vintage, and my friends often take a sip—as a humming bird drinks dew from a my cup.

We are creatures of habit, and, as the host, I enjoy offering my friends the hospitality of our home, simply good fellowship, complimentary to our understanding of social forms and so forth. This is bread. Its whiteness is like that of manna in Pharaoh's time, and it comes in the same fashion. Taste it? You recognize the faint sweetness.

Here are the boys in from a romp. These are William, Henry, Albert and Ambrose. We adopted four—you see, we like to have plenty of youngsters about.

They have organized a company and each evening they employ their time in drilling for service; for the armies here are mobilized and new recruits are added every day.

I am busy, myself, in helping Lloyd George, and the time is here for active service. Do you hear the thum-thum of the drums? The excitement is contagious— time is up.

CHAPTER XI
MESSAGE TO THE MOTHERS

February 7, 1917

The line of thought I wish to follow tonight is that of Preparedness. It is the essential thing in life, not only that of nations, but of individuals.

The fact of our existence is a thing beyond our comprehension. When a baby is born, the mother does not often enter into analytical thought concerning the destiny that caused his initiatory existence, neither does she often stop to think why he or she came; and seldom extends her thought to where he is going after he leaves the Birth Planet. She leaves this to circumstance—I am not censoring mothers—God forbid! But from my extended viewpoint, I have gained some knowledge of life, and its Purpose far in advance of my former knowledge.

To the mothers, I am speaking tonight. I am the living soul of a mortal body now passed into disuse. What I am, every soul will become in time. It is true that I am disengaged from mortal activities, so far as the world material is concerned, but when my mother gave birth to a child, she gave to the Universal Creation the highest form of creation—a man in embryo, imprinted with an indelible stamp. As to feature, race or nation, it matters little where I was born. The hut thatched and poor may usher its children into a palatial life. The future of the child is not determined so much by its environment, as by the thoughts and purposes of those who brought it into the world—if little or no thought is given to shaping the soul of the embryonic man, he becomes absorbed by whatever is given him for mental food—it is not necessary that mothers or guardians of the young should use the spoken or the vibrant voice. It is often better to speak in the silence, for tone sometimes absorbs thought and the intent is lost in bewilderment.

As love is felt in the presence of the home, and those who feel it bask in its radiance and energize, as plants in the sunshine growing into the full capacity of Being, so does hate or strife cripple and maim life and growth, like shadows in stale pools of unmoved waters. This is not hyperbole. It is Truth, faintly expressed.

Life in its relation to futurity should be the study of mankind. Various institutions of learning are abridging knowledge in adhering to doctrinal disputes in regard to what they please to call religious belief. In all kindness, I urge teachers and professors in schools and higher branches of educational work to disorganize branches where there is the ordinary theological stumbling block of debate.

Science and theology are related, relatively simple as grounds of a common universal knowledge. Educators often stamp themselves atheistic on general principles, which oppose religion, commonly on moral grounds, believing that religion introduces a higher moral standard than that of science. In the essential, both religion and science are scientific, operated by exact laws, simultaneously with each other. To avoid one, is to become crushed by the other, as the laws of the Universe work in relative correspondence, each expressing that for which it was originally set in operation.

The belief of the individual is not essential to the working or to the enactment of the law, so far as the law in regard to its effect is concerned. The sun revolves on its orbit whether I believe it or not. This is of no moment to the sun, but it is of vast importance to me, if I place myself as a barrier to the movement of the sun, I would be hurled to atoms in my futile attempt. To disbelieve what is unseen or unknown is radically foolish and does not in any sense excuse one from ignorance. I am writing as one who has gained his experience on the Other Side of life—to be imparted to those who have not given Life serious consideration, owing to lack of knowledge in regard to its continuity, believing that after death there will be no further use for the mind.

With the absolute knowledge of the Continuity of Life stamped on the individual mind, there will be a quickened impulse to command our forces, using them to broaden our understanding in our relation to home and to the social world in which we move, making society more suitable and habitable for the men and women contributing to its functions.

It is my wish to impress upon the student the imperative need of beginning the study of This Side of life by taking up the work in its initial stage—on the material plane of being—for as I have said before: Life is *one existence* before and after the great change.

Simply, your eyes are not attuned to tenuous matter, although your material body may sense it, and your soul explore, without difficulty, remote distances.

The object of this chapter is to direct the mind to the consideration of Life in the child; within its delicate organism is a complete creation. The Creator designed this jewel for the habitation of Eternal Existence in this world now, and by and by in a Universal World, beyond the comprehension of the mind at the earth stage of development. However, the creation is perfect, unless abnormality has interrupted the creative process. The brain cells contain the full cells for the cycle of life in uninterrupted creation. Man dwarfs his knowledge by not using to his capacity, his God-given implement of knowledge. For, within his own organism is resident full knowledge of Man, of Life, of Creation, of Destiny, Purpose, Action, Wisdom, etc. For Man contains in embryo the complete creation, awaiting development under his own masterful direction.

CHAPTER XII
THE MINISTRY OF HEAVEN:
OCCUPATION, ETC.

NEW YORK CITY
February 9, 1917

These are epoch-making days both in the material and the spiritual universe—the two are so closely blended. The mind is bathed in the ether of one, while the physical body receives nourishment from the other; both the mind and body are sustained by relative correspondence.

That which engages the public mind is incidental to that which the observer notes on This Side of the border. This is the point of progress for the ongoing thousands entering Eternity; a system is found at every port of entry; an absolute system under the dominion of laws built when the system of planetary creation evolved from chaotic nebulae into form under the control of the Omnipotent Power which we designate as God.

The laws are invisible but become a part of the student body curriculum. This is not arbitrary.

The mind clothed in the desires it brings with it readily absorbs whatever naturally belongs specially to its province, receiving therefore classification essentially to its choice. You will observe how varied are the classifications and how great the field of preference. There is nothing arbitrary and no compulsion or enforcement of laws—no laws broken—strict compliance with law as it is.

I do not intend to convey the idea that all are on the same level after having crossed the border of experience, but rather hope to make clear that what the soul brings of its attainments and culture while on the Birth Plane entitles that soul to its classification here; whatever that may be is established in the soul itself. His bar of judgment lies within himself. No accuser waits to condemn him. The veil that has obscured his vision of reality is gone. He observes his life as it is; he begins at once his work of restitution—sometimes from a very low plane. The eagerness of his desire accelerates his rise to higher planes.

There are numerous arrivals hourly when canvass is eagerly made for pleasure jaunts and for cards and for financial speculation. These scenes are daily panoramic—going and coming—before the eyes of those whose life absorbed such pursuits.

The immensity of space invites exploration, and after a while the earth soul becomes disenthralled and reaches through desire to higher levels.

The world here is actively engaged in exploration of space and discoverers are making charts of new systems of worlds, some of which have tenuous air valves; scientists are very interested in applying theories of invention.

Geologists are finding some new specimens of ore, resembling oxide of potassium, having as a base several carbonates containing stalactites of unusual brilliancy and color deeply shading into maroon.

Women come with baskets on their arms and gather up gems as one might pick berries in a swamp; some of them pave garden walks, and others make chains, while others are distributed along paths leading in directions where more may be found.

We become interior decorators after our own fashion, as everything is obtained for the searching. The nurses are making a salve and the battlefields are full of these gentle sisters administering to the wounded. No one is idle; reports are eagerly sought. Ships in disaster are signaled and many escape through our intervention. Lifeboats are kept afloat by those who go down to the waters to save boats, for many must not journey hence until life work there be accomplished. Those who come receive the Life Certificate, the victory over death.

The cycle changes. Indications fraught with powerful influences in Europe, betray a deep unrest in the heart of the people downtrodden and suppressed by false traditions; their eyes are opening to the depth of infamy disaster has supplied. The crucial test must be applied—dynasties must fall.

CHAPTER XIII
THE PLANETARY BALANCE

February 10, 1917

The interest of the world at this moment transcends that of any time since the beginning of creation, when worlds were hurled into space and empires were formed according to their several planetary locations, and nations arose and divided and subdivided and fought for preeminence among other nations. Nations subscribe arbitrarily to unwritten laws governing equilibrium, or balance, as written on the scales of planetary balance in the creative policies so wonderful in contemplation.

The work of creation involved the curriculum of universal knowledge in the application of higher mathematics, designed by Omnipotence to apply to all creation, bringing all together in harmonic relations as a whole creation. Calculus explains in part, in miniature, the process correlating under one common denominator, which includes in world processes of enumeration, geologic resistance, water pressure, gas expansion, mineral contraction and expansion, vegetable, mineral and animal creation, and inhibitory processes which must be included in the analysis.

The effect of magnetic attraction and deflection caused by other heavenly bodies in contra-distinction to our own has entered into the geometric calculation, in order to establish the system of worlds and the motor enginery of propelling them through space. There are people living on the Birth Planet today who proudly affirm that all this came by chance in the ordinary event of creation.

People become arrogant through the possession of worldly goods and honors conferred on them by state or nation, and believe themselves to belong to some higher order of creation yet to be awarded kingship—with this erroneous thought, self becomes highly magnified—the Creator is the nominal ruler only. The minds of the people become the ruling minds of the nation embodied in the governorship of king or emperor or ruler of whatsoever kind of administrative government. That the invisible reign of law includes the personality, all must admit, for we are made of the dust and with it we must return—I am now speaking of the material universe inhabited by coordinate beings—under the dominion of the universal laws governing planetary life and action. Man has not included himself in such laws to very great extent—but he has to such extent as to bring his home, his town, his city or nation into revolt with the system employed by the Master Builder of law and nations. Man is magnetic—he is born of dust, but "his brow is a searcher in the heavens, while his feet cleave to earth." Was it not the Concord sage who made this affirmation?

Ideas in multiform cause elation, depression, or loss of power. Either is within control of multiple of mind. Germany, staggering through the last century under the delusion of the greatness of her learning—and her advance in civilization—departed from belief in truth, swinging out of coordination with Law, blindly entering a war that must now go on until justice becomes established, regardless of consequences.

That other nations must suffer is natural to suppose. The correlation of empires of states includes the world's people, all brought out of position apart from coordination, out of orbits centrifugally, out of balance, endangering life and health. The magnetic attraction of bodies in coordination keep together, it is true, and when equality of balance is regained and harmony reigns, the world will have regained control of its path through the stars, clarified of greed to great extent, continuing its whirl through space with added souls watching for the dawn of peace eternal in the heavens. Earth is a good place to live in—but the real life is here. Earth is the type, the experimental stage. You know exactly what is meant by experience so far as you have lived. There you are the apprentice to your own soul—here you are the promoted individual. Nothing is left behind you worth anything. Gold you could not use if you brought it here—Love is the coin of exchange that you will bring with you. Bring all of your soul treasures— you will need them, your culture, your love of art, of music—all this you will use. "All things shall be given unto thee." Every want shall be satisfied. Material possessions you will not need.

CHAPTER XIV
THE SHINING LIGHTS OF HEAVEN

February 11, 1917

The avenues of the ethereal spaces invite adventure tonight. The light of day adorns the trysting places. For night, in relation to darkness, is unknown here. The radiance of light emanates from Being. We are all radiant indeed, in our veils of white, through which the radiance of our tenuous being flames forth a silvery light known as the Astral light.

We are undisguised, for on our foreheads is the insignia of whatever we have gained in culture, love for humanity, charity, selflessness, energy and force, ambitions for the sake of others—all this is here waiting for us when we are given our place in Heaven. For surely we are given our Price, our Wage, whatever we have earned during our years of apprenticeship.

Here run the rivers we love so well in Heaven. The atmosphere is so full of joy. It is Love that fills us to the height of adoration. The rivers, the light, the avenues, the work to do, the singing of the little ones by the way, the harmony, the grace of culture, the galleries of art— those masters of fame whose life work is left for those who have not yet attained. All this that I endeavor feebly to express is a part of our everyday experience.

The light that differentiates the hours from those of morning and night is tinted with amber, or light blue, gently diffusing through space golden glints of subdued light.

The index on our brow is not arbitrarily placed. We receive no stamp—the voice of Guardian Angel is unheard to say, come here, or go there. We, ourselves, do not see our own life index. The mark on our foreheads comes as our way we tread, looking for home or friends. The music, the light, the happiness we breathe, imparts to the newcomer great exhilaration— we are often unconscious of the change, as the blending of the seasons, the advance and the ebbing of the tide, the change of day into radiant twilight—so is the afterglow of the Life Transcendent.

To those of us who have attained and have found a way of expression, to those yet on the way up the Mountain of Experience, to those who are bringing their sheaves, I wish most profoundly to call halt, examine your treasures, look over your store of hoardings you are freighting to the unknown port. What you are bringing with you will be given to you for your inheritance—is here already, waiting for you. This is not religion, apart from science. It is written down in the Law of Human Life. You find whatever you search after. In all the category of experience, you gain what you are searching after—in literature, in art, knowledge, science, invention, love—attainment in culture, wisdom, riches or treasure, selfishness, etc. All is accorded you. The spiritual embodiment of your life work is your treasure in Heaven, those laid up by yourself, your treasures, your mansion, your reward for all you have done on the Earth Plane is laid up by yourself for yourself when at last you attain your reward for deeds done in the body. No arbitrary avenging angel awaits you. Creation afforded you, in the beginning, the implements of industrious labor to satisfy the craving of hunger of the body, and for the satisfaction of the soul. Within your complex organism the Creator placed a guide—your passport through the world and through eternity.

As the stars travel through space held within the confines of creation by laws inviolable—so man travels through his environment holding within himself the law of Being, the inexorable law of life which is continuous and masterful. He is himself the sovereign of his destiny, the master of his fate. Created in the Image of God, he is the Son of the Most High. Lighted by the lamp of conscience, he builds an empire within himself; his lordly possessions reach within to Infinitude; without are limitations of the physical—arrested at dissolution—no longer of use, returning into space through evaporation. Why has man proceeded so far on his way without recognition of his destiny, his inheritance with the eternal nature of things? His vista of mind has encircled the globe; he reaches out and girdles the earth with the strength of his thought—he speaks through the wind and his spoken word travels through spaces unharnessed by lines of travel. He rides the air and under the sea—he reads fates of nations in the stars—he subscribes to futurity the records of marvelous achievements, but of that which lies within himself, deeply imbedded within his inner life chambers, he wants not.

He does not understand that within are charts containing directions for his feet.

As if by chance he might forget
The way led upward to the Light
And traveled far;
Then lost in fog of doubt,
Confused,
And in the uncertainty mistake
The shifting day
For breakers on the way.

CHAPTER XV
MULTIPLE MIND—THE BIRTH OF AN IDEA

The process of analysis introducing phases of life, aside from that of exterior deductions, is extremely interesting to the student who is a searcher after truth. In this respect, analytical diagnosis is just beyond the veil of material sight—I may tell you of sights and scenes about me, describing journeys and painting for you the colors of flowers, and where to find hidden treasures, and all this. But to come to you with a strictly scientific analysis of the demonstration of laws beyond the plane of the ordinary mind, is evidence of my assertion of the continuity of life, as demonstrated in the substantial evidence of the correlation of parts of mind.

The mind of the student who reads this work, and that of the mind that expounds the Truth in reference to the inexplicable demonstrations of Truth, combine in elucidation of the problem. The two brains in correlation make the multiple mind, the unit of the mind, the whole mind. Your mind in conjunction with my mind, or that of some other mind on a similar plane, is necessary in order to maintain equilibrium of mind.

We are now in a color-tone susceptible of a very high vibratory tension. Your vibratory tone is dense compared with mine, in a higher tenuous form. The difference in tenuous vibration, and that of oracular, is adjusted by a curious process of physics, calculated to balance evenly the two minds in correlation. Absolute harmony of thought is the natural result. One thought form merges into other thought forms as the process of law develops. My brain pours into your brain, and in turn your brain ushers into mine the gray-matter substance converted into thought waves in correlation with those of mine. The law is now in operation. You have the ability to think the thoughts of God, after Him, in conformance to this law—your mind is therefore the mind of a god, analytical—powerful.

Men of powerful inventive genius such as Edison, have reached out in thought, in exploration of the unseen, and coupled with laws of correlation, unwittingly giving to the world secrets found in the brain of one advanced to the place of higher correlative thought. All advancement is made in this way, whatever that advancement may be, science discovery, invention. The unit of mind, the whole mind, creates the form created—a birth of an idea is ready for presentation to the world.

Truth is always established in this way. Christ's declaration of the lifted Christ drawing all men, is typical of the elimination of false belief, the magnetic attraction of Truth. The Serpent in the Wilderness is the same type of salvation through contact with Truth.

In this very manner will belief in the immortality of the soul receive confirmation. Man has within himself the power of correlation with Truth, which is the scientific demonstration of Truth capable of verification through experiments with the concrete, and therefore justified in the abstract, as well as law, is unfailing in its demonstration whenever set in motion. Therefore, to return to my premise, I regard the war as highly constructive inasmuch that what is false in belief will necessarily be eliminated from the minds of people out of correlation. Falsity vanishes when beaten or whipped out of power, there is no rock of defense; it simply evaporates as poisonous mind product, leaving Truth in the ascendant. There is no middle ground. Truth in the concrete is firm in fundamental structure.

Therefore, if you will kindly return to the introduction of this primary law, established between the lower and the higher tentacles of space, you will observe more minutely my meaning when I endeavor to point out the cause of this most unjust and unholy war in which the material will is in universal combat with the physical forces in correlation with the invisible world; that this unseen world should enter into correlation with the world engaged in mortal combat, is essential to the re-establishment of Truth, the elimination of false belief and the re-establishment of harmony, which is the planetary path which keeps in motion the stars and the worlds swinging through space.

The world conflict deflects the planetary system, causing in turn volcanic action, tidal waves, fires, earthquakes, and so forth. That this statement is true, may be verified by correlation of thought, by the student who strives to obtain Truth direct. "Ye shall know the truth, and the Truth shall make you free," is the most powerful utterance of Divinity.

None but God had measured the truth of this statement and the ages have come and gone—centuries have wrapped themselves within the folds of Infinitude and crept away in the shadows and still the thought of man has not grasped the truth of this statement.

The Nineteenth Century dawned and slipped within the heart of the Twentieth, and still man is unthinkingly wandering about in his swaddling clothes of ignorance.

This prophecy is now fulfilled—the peoples of the world emerging from the greatest war in the history of creation must throw off the mask of false teachings and lift up Its face unto the hills from where help comes.

The emancipation of the world typifies that scriptural new world where falsity will drop away like a garment and Truth will remain in transcendent beauty. Harmony will be the new Heaven. The old earth of bitterness will be revived by the Spirit of Love and Devotion.

CHAPTER XVI
THE ELEMENTAL DISASTER

NEW YORK CITY
February 14, 1917

The thought uppermost in my mind tonight is that of the warring nations. We are so closely connected with life in both planes that when thought is concentrated on one particular subject, we are magnetically drawn to the same thought and we mingle our thoughts with yours. These thoughts might easily be read by those who cultivated their sense of receptivity. The waters are exceedingly angry. The air about us is becoming more and more clouded. This is partly the apprehension of the people, as the situation becomes more tense. The conflict in the sea seems to be one of riotous savagery. People are swiftly leaving steamers and finding refuge in lifeboats. Others recede and are lost to sight for a few moments. Many are wafting about. Some little ones are clinging to their mothers' skirts and some families come together. Many aged people, also. With them are guides, whose duty it is to conduct them—all seem happy.

Many do not know where they are. Some think they have arrived at some foreign port. With you lies the tragedy of death—with us the happy awakening.

February 20, 1917

The world having set in motion forces that are tremendous in action, cannot control what has become a universal conglomerate of action, enveloping not only the earth itself, but the atmosphere surrounding the globe.

Every known living thing is absorbing the elemental disaster. The human families are not the only sufferers; the brute creation, the animal kingdom, the winged creatures, the mineral and vegetable creation all inhale and exhale the poison generated by hate. The Innocent must suffer. As the strife generated in the heart of those in high places, where culture and wealth, invention and ingenuity brought great riches, the mind of that ruler became imbued with the desire for greater influence, for more territory, for world power! His barns were full to repletion. The laws governing nations, he could overrule with his great power. He did not estimate the strength of the invisible laws under whose dominion he labored; thus, in his madness he struck the blow that toppled over the pinnacle of fame under which he stands today, committed to justice. The world shook at the dastard blow. Out of poise she travels through space, the stars shining obliquely in their gazing. There are other laws standing sentinel to those of justice. Out of the shadows comes the law of compensation and this law is upholding the arms of England and France—sustaining Belgium, strengthening and inspiring armies for the defense of justice. Compensation is unyielding in its demand. Justice must be satisfied, is written on her banners flung in the face of all civilized nations.

Arise, you men of civilization! It is not for the control of one nation, nor for the rage of mortal man. The world calls for justice—peace, peace!—the world calls loudly for peace. When there is no peace, justice must be satisfied, and in the eternal nature of things, the world will be purified as by fire. This is compensation. You are fighting for justice.

This happy awakening is undisturbed by visions of unreality. Life unfolds from the developed soul into the consciousness of a new experience vastly different from anything previously known. The degree of apprehension of the new life is commensurate to the preparation made while in the flesh. The perfect flower's form and texture grew into its loveliness through the preparation of culture for its peculiar and essential need. This preparation is the divine defense from the vegetable to the animal kingdom and beyond, to man, to his habitation, his empire, his country. You will see that this is logical. The United States lacks defense. The long years of peace have introduced a peaceable race. The peace-loving peoples of the world have flocked to America. The tactics of war have been neglected. Boys have been taught to abhor war and to keep the sword within the scabbard—a thing of historical interest to adorn the wall of some patriotic descendant. The nation has become highly civilized, educated, refined, cultured in philosophy and eminently classical—rich in science and invention. Peace has made this possible. The warlike nations do not evolve, only in extension of empire, never on higher planes. So, in contributing to the culture of world forces, the United States has declined in heroic ambitions, as a body politic. The organism is not military, save a highly decimated part. Military leaders are in the minority. There is no lack of patriotic fervor, but there is a great lack of patriotic power.

Since the days of Washington and Lincoln, the physical fiber of the human race has become enervated. Men have become softened by the life of ease, by non-resistance to climatic conditions. Living in steam- heated houses—sitting in the lap of luxury—results in ultra-conditions, the opposite of which are contrary to expediency. Patriotic zeal is there, but bodily tissue is not able to subscribe to the exactments of war. God pity the people remote from the elements. The Garden of Eden was the ideal dwelling for man. Man is a seasonable creature, designed by the creator to live in the open fields. Habits of luxury have inured him to ease and to warmth, because his powers of resistance have become less and less as civilization has brought him greater conveniences, which he has used so long that without these ends to comfort, his physical organization would perish in either extreme; moreover, he has placed his thoughts in defense of his position and no strong fleet or army stands between him and the enraged invader. Behold the preparedness of animal creation. Man, the highest of the animal kingdom, has sacrificed his coat of armor, his ability to fight the elements and in so do-ing has lessened his powers of resistance. Thus he in-variably reaches to his level in the inevitable struggle for supremacy in the world, for he is the master of his fate, the creator of his destiny. The race will be to the swift and to the strong. The conflict will be a bitter one, but the end will be a victory over maladjustment of life forces and the disintegrating process is necessary in the establishment of harmonic relationships in nations.

As in all phases of life, the weak suffer with the strong, the right with the wrong; this introduces a subtle reasoning that must be followed minutely and with exceeding painstaking thought, for it lies deep within the enlightened consciousness of the student of life forces in relation to extraneous forces correlating to those deeply imbedded within the human personality. In exact balance, according to the ratio of weights, determined by unseen but universal laws. The Bible is full of references on this subject.

CHAPTER XVII
IF A MAN DIES SHALL HE LIVE AGAIN?

NEW YORK CITY
February 16, 1917

Civil law is subject to discussion through arbitration pro and con. The best expert readers of law are secured to win the suit. It may be won by eloquence, or by failure to interpret the law, according to the statute books. Sometimes writers of law leave flaw-holes, crevices, capable of cleavage. Adroit lawyers sometimes take advantage, under cover of the law, to enrich their coffers, or to win plaudits from the most favored client. Juries often decide cases—there may be absolute justice accomplished and the guilty suffer; more often such is not the case, as the majority of my readers will affirm.

The subject I am about to lecture on this evening is analogous to the subject under consideration, viz., a point in law to be settled by arbitration.

The argument will be presented by one who has read Civil Law and who has conformed to its statutes during the period of his activity within the confines of materiality. During the years of his promotion to the Other Side of Life, the defendant gained knowledge in advance of the present time, and is prepared now to demonstrate by argument against argument, presented before the bar of justice in contradiction to any civil law exponent, who is prepared to enter the field controversy in regard to the question of Life Eternal.

I am more of a scientist than I am a lawyer and my thesis must be presented to the people in plain, intelligible type, that he who runs may read. For this is the first time in the history of the Universe that a challenge has been issued from outside the tenuous world of space in which immortal life extends to regions beyond the power of the mortal mind to contemplate, to the earth plane where millions are asking the question that must now be answered in a way that is convincing to the individual soul that is searching for truth. *If a man dies, shall he live again?*

First, the man does not *die*, for he is an immortal soul. You say this statement is theoretical— prove it; tell me what life is. You affirm that you do not know. Is it electrical?

Physicians have demonstrated the body compound and assert that it is dissoluble matter, and soon evaporates and disintegrates. It is matter built into the most delicate tissue, through which it functions through initial activities. Is the soul able to rehabilitate itself after its initial dishabilament, in casting aside its flesh? It is clothed in immortality. When does the soul gather unto itself its garment of immortality? When life is given to the babe, the robe of immortality is the gift of God, indicative of kingship.

How may we know that what you say is true?

This may be revealed through the gift of the Holy Spirit. Seek, and ye shall find.

But I cannot believe that which my eyes cannot see or my hands feel. Granted, then; to supplement this need of materiality, God has established a route of demarcation to such travel according to sight and touch. This route reaches through space; well-worn is the path, for the thought of man leaves grooves in the eons of space; the path is of easy access to those who would travel. *This is Faith.* Paul called it "my shield and buckler." The world needs it today. "Your eyes cannot see, nor your hands touch."

Think a moment of what I am about to say. Where are you standing this moment? If on the street, what do you see? As far as your eyesight reaches—what is beyond, travel demonstrates. All this is obvious. Atmospheric conditions render the air invisible to eyes attenuated to earth vibrations; eyes, however, are not the only organs of sense. Intuitions often apprise us of the approach of one attenuated to higher vibratory life. This is sense, and is capable of accurate analysis.

Touch is inevitable, for we move within each other's spheres incognito. Much is apprehended that escapes comprehension, for lack of enlarged cellular development. This brain culture must be from within. All culture is obtained through the development of special brain cells adapted to certain phases of culture. The artist who is searching for tints expressive of sunsets does not wish them mingled with architectural designs or aerial charts—neither does the statesman care for inventions of electricity to interfere with his politics.

The highly organized brain has enough capacity for the use of the individual soul during the term of its immortal existence through the ages of time extending into infinitude.

Man's opportunity is abridged because of his misunderstanding of himself as an immortal entity. His plan has been to die with his body. The shadowy lights thrown on the screen, giving him glimpses of the hereafter, have not been sufficiently intelligible as to satisfy his cravings for knowledge. Nor is it at all strange—the fact that man is still searching for Truth is evidence that Truth has not yet appeared to his expectant mind. The lover, when he finds his mate, is satisfied—his heart is at rest—love knows its own. This is *prima facie* evidence of the fact that love has been found.

When Truth dawns on the world in all her beauty, then shall the mind of man be satisfied, because the receptivity of Truth will come to occupy the soul of man still waiting for Truth. This is *prima facie* evidence. When Truth is received, then shall the heart of man be satisfied, for it shall then see its last endowment of culture and become the unit of soul, perfect as the man, Christ Jesus. "Ye shall know the truth and the truth shall make you free."

CHAPTER XVIII
THE FAMILY UNIT

NEW YORK CITY
February 18, 1917

Those who object to the occasional Scripture quotation must be resigned to their fate—there is no middle ground. I cannot lecture on immortality from these celestial heights without the Word of God in my heart and on my lips. From Him I received my immortal spirit, and to Him I owe my allegiance. From Him I received my inheritance of culture—what little I possess. To those who are hungering for the truth, I would be wrong to withhold what I know to satisfy a criminal desire for ignorance of truth in the atheistic or infidel mind.

What I say, I say clearly. I am not here to employ ambiguous language or technical terms in describing a life inhabiting two sides of existence. Please take note; I say a life inhabiting two sides of existence.

There have been no changes in creation of the human family. This is the ordained creation of man. The old doctrinal idea that at death a new body containing new sets of faculties, was given us, is erroneous.

God's creation of man was complete in the beginning without interruption. Man proceeds into his complete existence at the termination of his career here, going back as a developed soul, wearing his robe of immortality, the precious gift he brought with him through his mother's soul. Thus are family ties holy and sacred in their unity. This is why the children cling more to mother. May I say to motherhood: Guard your immortal souls, for into life goes the babe, wrapped within the folds of your spirit. Keep motherhood holy.

The curious mind has developed a fantasy for exploring the tenuous atmosphere connecting the sphere above.

Inquisitiveness is a highly organized human faculty, for we are all human. We are not less human after our promotion to a higher sphere, connected with the lower plane. Kindly note the differentiation of the *higher sphere* and the *lower plane.* The correlation is exact with that of the human personality: the material and spiritual, two in one.

Through the range of creation, God has endowed his creatures with a love of the same kind, from the creation of the human family to that of the animal, and from thence to the vegetable creation. All are grouped in family circles; even trees of the forest find family relationship in establishing within groups the younger branches, offshoots from the parent trees.

CHAPTER XIX
THE NEW ERA OF PSYCHICAL
RESEARCH

NEW YORK CITY
February 18, 1917

Stars travel through space in family groups. The Pleiades are examples—the Seven Sisters, carrying their sweet influences—"Can you bind the sweet influence of the Pleiades, or break the bands of Orion?" writes Job, who read the mysteries of the stars.

The earth and heaven is but another example of this axiomatic truth. But you will say, what of the other worlds and systems of worlds traveling through space? How is it that this earth planet is so favored?

Here is the secret of Godship; it is not the province of this book to repeat all that is written. There is much yet to be revealed, and God will lead us there from time to time, as the mind of man inquires.

Today we have reached a new era in the field of discovery. Previously the way was veiled. There was very little written in the light of the revealed consciousness under normal conditions. Abnormality has had its night; its province must cease with the ushering in of a new day in the full glare of the noontide sun. There need not be the abnormal, the supernormal, the subnormal consciousness; the pendulum of consciousness has been swinging far into the midnight and far out of position beyond the daylight, in the endeavor to establish equilibrium. At last equilibrium is established and the safe route from the upper sphere to the lower plane accomplished.

The traveler who employs this route will not be startled by the dim appearance of shadows lurking to intercept him or to thwart his efforts—for in his future investigations he will employ only the normal agency of that law developed within himself by the enlargement of cell-capacity.

As time hastens on toward the future, the tenuity of the atmosphere will become more in accord with that of the lower plane, because of the influx of thought vibrations invading new channels of the dense atmosphere. This is the inevitable result.

As the world is suffering today through discord and hate, plunging through space out of its regular line of travel, so will the future see the two spheres, the upper and the lower, bound together in one atmosphere, one heaven, one earth, reunited through harmony and love. Then shall men see face to face, even as we are seen.

You will observe that the cultivation of the occult forces within you is unnecessary to the enlightenment of the coming age. The brain now employed becomes dull to the finer vibrations; having attached itself to abnormal atmospheric conditions it receives false, unreliable impressions. Some phenomena have been attained by the forced intermingling of atmospheres— but the results are highly injurious to those who bring about such results, and for no special gain save that of a morbid curiosity.

Therefore I urge the student of life seeking after Truth to avoid obtaining it in such an abnormal, illusory manner. Within every human organism there lies a highly sensitized reflectograph. As the heart is guarded within the structure of the body, so is this sensitized faculty of the mind guarded deeply within the cellular tissues of the brain, when discovered through culture of faculty. The brilliancy of this faculty is enhanced by that of other cell culture in close proximity; through attention and close application to the interior development of this discovered faculty, satisfactory results may be obtained in connecting thought and assured correspondence through the two atmospheres.

It is a lamentable truth that those who have been promoted to the Higher Sphere of life should suffer the ignominy of the Lower Plane's thought following them into this higher existence in vapor-like substance, more like material atmosphere, every known epithet hurled after them.

This evidence of the ignorance of the Lower Plane seems inexcusable, as science and invention have coupled the thoughts of men with the stars.

Conservatism still holds its band between civilization and the light beyond.

Occasionally a courageous spirit advances and lifts the veil and comes back with authentic reports; not the obnoxious veil of abnormality, but the lifted veil, revealing divine faculty, normally expressed. I bid all such God-speed.

CHAPTER XX
THE MASTER CREATION: THE PROMISE

February 18, 1917

Note with vibrant joy the change in the heart of man under the stress of the war conditions and that of the inquiring mind in regard to God's will in allowing the holocaust that bids fair to envelope the two hemispheres, to continue.

Man, the Masterpiece of Creation, endowed with every faculty, has been given pre-eminence in creation. His position in the universe is a little lower than the angels, all things have been placed beneath his feet; "the birds of the air, the fish of the sea, yea, whatsoever passes through the paths of the sea."

In reviewing man's achievements during the present century, we are prepared to believe that God made no mistake in his estimate of the man whom he first made out of clay and endowed with the breath of Life, establishing him on the invisible throne of his destiny—here man begins his reign over self and over his own environment, coexistent with his individual appointment. To be conserved by his Creator, to be led by a chain, to be tied to a rock, to be enjoined in action, or to be coerced or thwarted in his leadership would be the work of a human, not a Divine Master.

He has been richly endowed by an inexplicable endowment of faculties for every demand of his material and spiritual nature. He has also been given a library of reference more profound in learning than any other book the world has ever known. In this Book lies his A, B, C of culture, of life, character, decision, of whatsoever nature his chart, his compass, his route leading through the complex path he must needs tread away unto the Celestial City.

The possession of this treasure at last satiates the appetite and after studying the Book for a while, man became anxious to write a treatise of his own, a chart better adapted to another route on which he would feign journey; so he has laid The Book aside and in so doing, lost his Guide. After centuries struggling through the dark—through splendid courts of earthly empire, accepting the plaudits of the people, he becomes his own guide and forgets that there was One who Is Guide to the Wayfarer. Suddenly catastrophe comes. He feels himself enveloped helplessly, his friends dying in battle, his country defeated, himself lost in calamity. Where is God? he cries hoarsely—the Saviour of mankind—where is He who said, "Behold, I am with you always—even to the end of the world"?

But you say, what of the believers? What of the innocents, the women, and the little children? Herein lies the tragedy of what seems remorseless fate, that the angels do not intercept the coming squadrons with swift pinions and stay the guns from their terrible onslaught. The laws of harmony have been swept aside. Man has placed himself in the firing line, under the inexorable conditions brought about by his own disobedience of law. Herein lies the fallacy of man's judgment. But "what is man's infirmity is God's opportunity."

February 19, 1917

There are those who discourage young people from undertaking military training, making the assertion that it presages war and incites in men military ambitions. Look over the various fields of action in Europe and in this country today and count the men who are beyond the age of thirty or forty years old who are leaders in the activities of state who have not received their training and preparation for statesmanship in some military academy, or where the study of military tactics has been encouraged.

The battle is to the strong. The fields of Europe are strewn with the brave young lads who gave to their country all they had, and certainly the preparation of the European citizenship in times of peace was infinitely more than that of the United States in this most critical time of her history. I use this as an illustration of what I am about to say to you at an hour when the forecast of the future of this country is imperiled, because of a lack of preparedness. What goes on in the world so far as those of us who are little removed from its anxieties, is of little consequence, so far as it concerns our individual interests. But I stand tonight on the confines of creation, viewing the awful spectacle the world presents to the view of all on this Upper Sphere, and as we gaze below, a tremor of grief spreads from man to man; women are gathered here in little groups, wringing their hands in an agony of heart, wishing there could be some palliating power—some relief given. But it seems that our ministrations should be given to the living, as well as to those who are coming in such large armies to recruit the armies here. We reach out our arms; and our prayers are comforting to those who suffer. But we realize that there is little more that we may do, as justice is unsatisfied and wrong unrequited.

It has become a war of civilization against barbarian agencies. The earth has slipped back into medieval history—this history of the past has been forgotten in the splendid advance of civilization. The history of the Roman Empire, of the Ptolemies, of the Egyptian dynasties, of Babylon and the archives of the great, found in the ruins of Pompeii, all prove that world chaotic forces swinging in one gigantic pile can wreck the greatest civilization the world has ever known!

When the rainbow spread across the sky after the first great upheaval of natural forces, covering the first world catastrophe underneath the waters, the Lord promised never to destroy the earth by water again. The promise of the Lord is remembered each time we view the harmony of colors we see mingling together in one splendid arch across the horizon. With this wonderful bow of promise, God introduced a spiritual law interwoven in the tints, mingling together so harmoniously, and this spiritual law governs the harmony of the peoples of the world; as the tints are mingled together in the bow of promise, so is the evidence of harmony written in the skies within the promise God gave to the world when he gathered the waters together and promised nevermore to destroy the earth. The world will not be destroyed—but this last great conflict will be the last one to mar the beauty of creation. From out the chaos of misery and disintegration, there shall come men and women, whose hearts shall be more attentive to the Voice of God.

The rainbow of promise still flings its banner of harmony across the horizon, and people beholding it, shall remember God and his infinite love.

The love of power and the love of gain shall be swept away in the debris, the new people shall love knowledge and study with understanding. Power will come, peace, right and justice shall rule kingdoms and principalities and there shall be no more war.

CHAPTER XXI
MEMORIES OF CHILDHOOD:
COMPANIONSHIP

February 20, 1917

There is a little playmate of mine with me tonight. We strolled along the path together, talking of the things we see. He sorrows much for those whom he left a year ago, and he tells me his dog, Bruno, came after him whining, and he wants Bruno.

This little chap lived in Missouri, he tells me. His name is Henry Willis Dwight. We get along well together, and the little one plays by my side and is now content and happy. He is much interested in this visit. He watches intently every movement of the pen, and reads my thoughts as you imprint them on the page. This is indeed a mystery to Henry for he does not see my lips move—and while he readily understands my unspoken thought, he cannot quite comprehend how you are able to do likewise. I have explained it to him, and tell him that to enter the Subway and take a train to Chicago or Washington would make no difference; that I do not often visit New York, but usually compile my data from some distant star or planet.

Coming along the path, Henry discovered ants crawling along the sand hills. He told me they were like emigrants, hiking bundles. He wanted to know what the ant did to sluggards, evidently trying to make some connection—I might have told him the ant carried his bundle, while the sluggard let somebody else carry his.

"Boy Scouts never do," promptly replied Henry.

"Bless you, no, my boy. Boy Scouts get many ideas from the little field heroes found everywhere in thrifty enterprises—no stagnation in the forests—everywhere active. At dawn all creation is up and at work. The birds, singing on their way, going south for the winter, or   returning north for the summer, building or garnering."

"Tell me, when you were a boy like me."

"All right, my lad. Sit here by my side while I tell you what I mostly enjoyed. When I was a boy, Nature held much for me. The trees in nutting time employed much of my time. I gathered the fruit and spread out the kernels in attic corners. The spiders that I met there created in me many venturous schemes. Those attic pirates? The beetles, moths and the bats—to be hit in the face by a bat in the dark is a rare bit of experience in a boy's memory.

How I loved to poke away those long, white, baby rattles hanging from the old rafters! Gee whiz! I remember the sting yet. Bluebottle flies, with that peculiar iridescent wing tissue, were most fascinating to me. Hornets and pinch-bugs won a great deal of sympathy, I guess because all the boys chased them and tried to kill them. . ."

Henry interrupted here and said, "Once I told a boy if he chased any more hornets, I would lick

him—I like hornets a good deal better than mosqui-
toes, their buzz is bigger and it gives a feller a chance
to get away. Once I found a beehive in a tree. Jimmy
Thurlow had a saw with him—we had been in Dad's
timber pile where we used to get blocks to make into
rafts to float down the stream where beavers used to
live. Jimmy said he wasn't afraid of bees; so he
took the saw, while I climbed up the tree beyond
where Jimmy sawed—Tell you! I thought my time
had come, when Jimmy opened up that hole. Jimmy
got it more than me. The bees just went for him. But
mother piled on tobacco and gave him most of the
honey. I'm glad she did. Bruno just saved his life by
fighting those bees and lashing them with his tail.
Bruno—Bruno—. . ."

"Henry, do you remember seeing the lady-
bugs and crickets in your garden, and the katydids at
twilight, singing at the door?"

"Yes, and one night I flopped a tree-toad from
my pillow, and another time killed a snake near the
well."

"Do you think a hornet is better than a
snake?"

"Well, a feller likes to defend something, but
no boy could stand up for a snake, 'specially a scout
like me."

CHAPTER XXII
THE RELATIONSHIP OF GOD TO MAN

NEW YORK CITY
February 24, 1917

There are many truths to be revealed in regard to Scripture that have not been interpreted by many, owing to the material development beyond that of spiritual mind.

The objective mind has been employed in the affairs of life on the plane of its activity, leaving the subliminal mind undirected and waiting its opportunity of expression. This is largely due to the general disuse of the Bible as the guidebook for which it was given to man.

The Scriptures are full of wisdom not beyond the understanding of men developed into the full stature of men. Will the student kindly follow my thought, patiently endeavoring to obtain its full meaning? This may not appear directly. Think deeply of what I am about to express, even though it appears to be abstruse.

Therein lies the secret, the revealment of which will give man the assurance of Truth related to himself, connecting him with the Universal Mind, God.

The Bible is the torch the enlightened mind may use in its search after Truth, correlating the mind with God; making that multiple of mind which is the prime essential; to those interested in the study of the human personality, this is the only way to Truth. The acceptance must come through that of the personal experience, as typified by the Scriptural references accessible to all that labor for the attainment of wisdom.

The mind urged by the intensity of desire responds to the accepted promise of God for wisdom and understanding. Thought becomes imbued with the idea of direction and the fact of experience as final in its discovery of the law by which certainty is reached.

Man has at last discovered himself, in his resident God-power, as the instrument through which God works out His plans through the human personality. To recognize and to apply this power is to gain wisdom and understanding. God is the power; man the instrument.

The conflict of opinion is so great in the world in regard to the future existence that it seems expedient for one who has entered into that experience to use every effort within his power to make conditions plain. I realize at once there will be a conflict of opinion. Those who refuse to believe the truth will also disbelieve my ability to transverse the realms of space and therefore express opinion.

I make no apology; to students and those who are earnestly seeking Eternal Life, I have worlds of comfort to impart. I speak with authority of one who has discovered treasure and hastens to lay his precious gems at the feet of those who perish.

This necessitates some revealment of the Bible riches and their relation to human need and enlightenment through application and the acceptance of Truth.

As the relation of man to the Infinite has been described in these pages, you will readily see that cutting off our source of supply brings disaster to us living in the physical universe. We are not aware, some of us who are not studious of affairs relating to the Life Beyond, that strict attention must be paid to the Word of God. It is our sure defense; it is life both in the abstract and in the concrete; it embraces all human experience; within the Word we find the Way and the Truth.

The way opens now for the revelation of some of the secret processes of powers within the human personality, so remote within the soul as to have evaded the research of ages.

Everything that is created is in accord with laws governing that special creation.

God ordains that his people should dwell in families; even the brute creation is not overlooked in this divine ordinance. The thought suggests great beauty in its coordination. From the reference, "to the fall of the sparrow," and "the numbering of the hairs of the head," implying the minute oversight—"the tender care of the Shepherd," all suggest the tender care of the Heavenly Father for the creatures of his own creation.

Centuries passed and man forgot his inheritance—his treasure hidden away—he has become a wanderer in his father's vineyard, a stranger from home. Disaster comes; he feels the earth falling away beneath his feet; gladly would he find his way. Some have learned the Way and are comforted in the thought. To those who have yet to find it, let me say that prayer is more than vain repetition of words, when we pray sincerely. This I learned in part before coming, here, as many others have done. What I then learned, I now verify as truth. The Father hears the faintest cry of his child; the answer is not always in accord with the preference of the child, but according to the best interests of that child's development.

This is the established relationship of God, the Father, to humanity. Every soul born into the earth plane is connected by right of divinity to the soul of God, the Father. This is your birthright, whether you recognize or accept your divine sonship or not. The gift belongs to you; the rich, the poor, the strong, the feeble, the alien—all are Sons of the Most High, Princes and Heirs to His Kingdom.

The earth, your birth plane, is your preparation for the affairs of the Everlasting Kingdom of Your Father who so richly endowed you with faculty.

"What is man, that you are mindful of him, or the son of man that you visit him? Thou hast made him little lower than the angels. You put all things under his feet: the fish of the sea, yea, whatsoever passes through the paths of the sea."

This rich endowment has been disbelieved and underestimated as fable or fairy tale. However, the fact remains, and man is still amenable to the laws ordained at the creation, whether he recognizes these laws or not.

Therefore, man is under the law and himself relatively connected with this same law; he may conform to its privileges, advancing him to higher levels, or ignore his masterful inheritance and sink to the level of his ambitions.

To those who strive for the mastery of self, the Bible contains invaluable hints of some hidden treasure which search may reveal.

These hidden treasures are found in the human personality when it becomes one with the Infinite.

The mind of man reaches out in search of God, who is attuned to his cry. "My sheep know my voice; I am the Good Shepherd and know my sheep and am known of mine."

This reference is important in enabling the student to understand the relation of the Heavenly Father to the child, symbolized in the tender Shepherd. Herein is the law exemplified and is in direct action today.

Prayer brings your mind into immediate contact with the Mind of God—your mind and the Mind of God unite in the Unit or multiple mind which is the basic principle of completeness. Herein lies your power with God, given to you unreservedly, so far as you are capacitated in receiving the blessing.

To those who have discovered their power through earnest search after the treasure, there are still open to their entranced vision vistas of experience exceeding great riches.

The forces of the world material are now getting evidence of the past. The wreck of the present seems deeper than the apathy of nations seems to realize. The world is moving rapidly toward the New Era—toward the dawn of that Perfect Day of reconstruction.

I do not wish now to use my golden hours in writing of the development of the illuminated prophecies of Old—recorded in the sacred Scriptures. Time and events are within a system of laws governing futurity.

It is my desire to present Truth to the receptive mind of the world in its entirety, concerning the human personality and its relation to God through the correlation of laws set in motion at the time of creation—at the same time to connect man as a moral entity independent in his material being, having the power of initiative and of free will.

CHAPTER XXIII
LOVE

The subject near my heart tonight as my glance sweeps o'er this stricken earth is Love.

The air is luminous with love, borne from This Side to that Other Side, falling through the medium of Hate. Here all is Love; and we have love in great abundance. The battlefields are strewn with the strength and the youth of Europe. All who are yet breathing the sordid smoke of battle are bathed in the atmosphere of love. The manly breast carried love into the fight and it was for love of country that he went courageously to die. Ah! He dies not alone. Angelic presences are near, breathing into his ebbing life the love of Heaven, mingled with his love of country, of home and loved ones. It is love that bears him and his comrades in arms to the Light that fades not away.

At creation, this place where we all come sooner or later was set aside for the wayfarer, those for whom the destiny of time and fate sent thither. "Eye hath not seen, neither hath it entered into the heart of man, the glories that await him."

This heaven is so close akin to my subject that herein may it be classed together with its twin-sister, Love. For Love is Heaven, and Heaven is Love. The angel closed the gate and stands sentinel, that hate may not enter in, to disturb Love and Harmony. Hate proceeds on her way with her comrades in chains of delusion and false belief, until at last this restoring, creative force absorbs and recreates them—for Love is compelling as Heaven is justice; and some there are who never heard of that Love which is God; for Love suffers long and is kind.

Love is the initial creation. God is the embodiment of Love, the essence of Love permeating all creation. I find imprinted on the brain of my correspondent, a definition of God. None better could be given, as this definition was given by the correlation of mind through prayer and definitely understood and written down years ago by my correspondent:

"I am Love, the Divine Essence of Life,
The Essence of Love radiating from my personality
Is Life to the world; the regenerating Power
Of this earth, the habilament of all verdure,
The Glory of all that exists."

God reveals himself to those who search earnestly to find him in the avenues of prayer. That to search is to find, is a self-evident proposition. God has given us minute directions in the chart he has left. "Seek and ye shall find" is not theoretical language.

The avenues of prayer must be kept unobstructed, leading to the mercy-seat. The world is turning eagerly in this direction. It is insecure; men seem to be moving about as dazed creatures, devoid of the mastery of mind. Men in high places are robed in veils—they do not see clearly. The unprecedented dazzles the brain. They stagger beneath the burden of government. They reel, knowing not which way to turn. The avenues of prayer grow branches of doubt which obscure the light beyond. Christians are sending prayers; I see the waves of light ascend. These are aerial messages, freighted with love for those who bend deeply over the intricate problems of the hour. Listen: the answers are sent back; the Infinite Mind controls them—listen to the still small voice. Dissociate all thoughts of the world for the moment—cultivate patiently the faculty of concentration. The gift belongs to you to cultivate.

This preamble to earthly love is the highest of all loves, for it is the brooding love of the Creator for the creature. Speaking with authority as one who discerns the creation from the advancement of life, I must employ the language best suited to express my meaning, for it is relative to the Mind of God when He created man in His own image and thrilled Him with the divine breath of Being which is love. This is the tie that binds the creature man to God, as a part of God, having within his soul the elemental essence of creation. Man may accept this thesis or not, refusing in his belief his power to love his wife, his children, through God. He cannot escape his divine prerogative. For in Him he lives and moves and has his being.

Love is the atmosphere of Heaven; we breathe none other; we are bathed in its effulgence. It radiates light; it is the dynamic force that moves worlds in space and stars in their courses; it is the creative essence; the new world, the new stars evolve through the force of love. The spring is the symbol of love. Here the young maiden puts on her glorious garment of green and brings forth the blossoms of her youth and understanding. The young feel the vitalizing power. The birds trill to their mates, and the nesting season begins.

Love is the master-painter of sky and landscape; of mountains and sea. The secret places He illuminates with the banner of His face. He touches all hearts with the rosy hue of His brush. The fields he spreads with the dew of His breath. The animals He touches with pathetic languor; they feel the divine impetus, and lie down with the calf.

Love is pure, is spiritual, and of Heaven, surviving bodily death. Passion is gross matter. Some blindly relate this to love. Passion is material, easily diverted temporarily on the side of love, capable of quick revulsion, to indifference or hate. It is distinctly separate from love, and has no relation to the Divine Essence. Passion satiates, disintegrates and does not survive bodily death.

Love is Life, both sides of life—the unit of life; the comeliest of all the personality, for it stamps the human with the Divine.

CHAPTER XXIV
MARRIAGE

NEW YORK CITY
February 27, 1917

Marriage is the uniting of twin souls. This is the only spiritual marriage and the only marriage that survives bodily death. This is a broad statement, but it will be substantiated by truth when perceived in relation to sex in the extended view-point of the student.

Throughout the universal creation, sex seeks completion in mating; in lower creatures, instinct leads to the choice and is followed by the amours of love responding to the laws of reproduction.

Material creation follows the laws of reproduction in vegetable product, in forestry, in flowers. The shells of the sea contain twin embryo, while the stars travel through space in quest of love.

The design in creation is that of harmony in detail. Here, in meditation, is the observer thrilled with the revelation in all of its singular fitness and beauty.

Truly is Paradise the central thought of creation, from out of this center of the human race radiates the grandest view ever presented to the world. Perfection in its entirety. Spirit and matter. The divine origin of man and his companion, woman: "bone of my bones, and flesh of my flesh." This creation typifies the relationship between man and wife.

The oneness of marriage is the essential to harmony, and therefore to family life, indispensable. The cradle of the human family was wrought in perfection, calculated to preserve the beauty of the form divine; of the sanctity of love the world is deeply cognizant; of all the mistakes and the sorrows of ill-guided unions and unhappy homes, of illegitimate children defrauded of their just heritage, of all that make up the sorrows of life, this is the most lamentable and far-reaching in its effect on life and society. Degeneration of the human race is inevitable when marriage is debased, for out of the consecrated home comes strength and fortitude for whatsoever life offers to man.

Chastity is the morning star lighting the castle and the cabin with rays of hope for the future of men and women. Without this the man degenerates in body and soul, to become incapacitated.

The years of degeneration have produced a dullness of apprehension in the human family, obliterating and stultifying nature's call, so that the riot of blood coursing through the veins of adolescent man, slow to maturity, develops within him unnatural desires, which he mistakes for love.

Love is spiritual, and in its truest embodiment brings into life, heaven, which it creates. This is the marriage which survives bodily death. They shall be one flesh, one spirit, one mind.

The multiple mind transcends the material existence. The two souls blend into one soul. There shall be no marriage in Heaven—because Nature is the minister of the human family, uniting souls destined to be one. Each soul has its twin soul. Cohesion attracts and unites them, as the dawn blends into the day.

Having lost the way, the human family must be guided by the laws of state or of nation in their preservation of law and of order, for the protection of purity and justice, the establishment of home and happiness in wedded love.

CHAPTER XXV
HEAVEN

NEW YORK CITY
March 8, 1917

Speculation attaches to the place of Heaven. When a boy, I thought Heaven to be a place in a far-off corner of the universe, enclosed within a high wall, so high and broad that none might break within the pearly gates; I imagined streets of gold and palaces of alabaster and a throne where God sat and administered justice, with attendant angels coming and going, with seats of preferment on either side of the throne; where choirs of angels sang praises day and night.

Today as I look about the place called Heaven, I see no such reminders of my childhood's imaginings. What I see is a vast expanse of area, illimitable. My vision extends to a place where I see a gentle decline—maybe several thousands of miles away. Everything swinging in space is spherical. Heaven is the exterior, or largest of all the system of planets within the universe—encircling all systems of creation, worlds and worlds, suns, empire of suns, stars and nebulae. All of this spherical creation travels within the orbit of its own path, carrying its special atmosphere constituted to the need of its habitant.

While the atmosphere of the heavenly sphere commingles with that of millions of worlds swinging within the heavenly sphere, it is not affected by contact

with extraneous atmosphere, as the tenuous air trans-
fuses while it does not absorb. Elimination of noxious
thoughts adhering to spirit gradually disperse in the extraneous. Jerusalem is the earthly type of this city, as
John saw it, coming down from God out of Heaven,
prepared as a bride adorned for her husband.

March 13, 1917

The opportunity is much appreciated.

I long to tell you more and more of this beautiful world in which I live, and the joys of life here. I
wish to paint in truth the Heaven I live in, that the pic-
ture may prove to be alluring to men and women on the
Earth Plane who ignore the fact of Eternity and join in
the pursuit of pleasure and forgetfulness at the expense
of their own salvation.

This is no idle dream or fantasy of the moment.
The windows of Heaven are open to the world and he
who is willing to look may see the fulfillment of prophecy in the events transpiring. The world in conflict!
Students, men of science, preachers and teachers of the
word, listen! Listen! Watchman, what of the night?
What are the signs of the coming of the Lord? Do the
men of the world forget their cunning? Their towers of
Babel sway in the morning. Wise men are thinking of
the time and of the promise and are questioning together the meaning of all this. Look back over the centuries
of darkness gradually leading up to the brilliancy of the
present age. Note the achievement and the sudden emp-
tying of the vast hidden treasure of discovery. This

means the end of the journey—the reaper is gathering up the sheaves of the harvest and is garnering them into the storehouse.

I would that I might use my power so generously afforded me now to invite men to a serious consideration of this message, in connection with the events transpiring in the world today.

Come now, let us reason together, as men grown to the full attainment of Being; the words abide within the secret place; the key to this has been given in the Book of Books and left for the interpretation of the nations. God broods over his people with the tender compassion of Fatherhood—the sorrows of the world, the groaning of the oppressed is wrought in love of the Father and enwrapped in his mercy.

From the viewpoint of man under the full stature of Being, the analytical love of God cannot brood over suffering; to Him God is away on a journey and fled, while the household is given over to the ravenous wolves. Not so, not so! God is in the storm, near the stricken fold, ministering to His children, enfolding them within His abiding Love. It is not death, to die. Our viewpoint is changed as we merge into the full stature of Being and we behold perfection as it is.

To you who gaze as through a glass darkly, it seems the iconoclasm of fate—the absolute disaster! This human struggle that staggers the imagination! The brute creation evolving on the fringe of civilization, eating its way down into the abyss of another cycle.

The weaver's shuttle moves swiftly, entwining the bright warp and the somber woof, the sunshine and shadow, the morning and the night, the twilight—the dawn, the storm—the calm, the heights—the depths, the spring and fall, the summer and winter, joy and sorrow. All this is balance—in other words, compensation: the unit of Life, the unit of Creation, the twinship of experience, wrought out of the vicissitudes of life.

Balance is essential, whatever the nature of the creation, whether it be still life, or vibrant in action. The Law is unstayed in its action, unthwarted in its advance through its channel cut deep in the world grooves; unswayed by empires or worlds hurtling through space out of orbit in the path of the destroyer— the Law works no ill.

"The voice of one crying in the wilderness 'make straight the path of the Lord,' " is today heard in the courts of the Most High. The ministry of the church hears the voice, and the people are advancing into the highways and repairing the broken places on the way, and placing lights in dark places. Men are aware of God's presence.

Maidens are trimming their lamps and adorning for the coming of the Bridegroom. Men are hastening in their effort to obtain wealth. "Make straight the path of the Lord."

March 16, 1917

The mind cannot conceive the splendors that await revealment. In justice to my efforts to describe the heavenly home, I must repeat, as I so often have said in the preceding chapters, that the personality gleans much of heaven while journeying remotely—what heaven is to me, measures up to my attainment there. I would that my language might be very clear—that no doubt should mingle with the Truth as I desire to express it.

My interior development intensifies the beauty and the glory of Heaven. My soul is Heaven in embryo—his is the same of every soul—God created man in His own Image. As the soul becomes luminant in understanding, Heaven is revealed; the eyes, those windows of the soul, reveal the kingly dwelling place within: the Temple of the Holy Spirit abiding: the dwelling place of the Most High, God!

This is not figurative language. It is old as the Word given to Moses on the tablet of stone. I am privileged to turn the light on the pages after many centuries have crept down the ages, wrapped in the swaddling clothes of oblivion. The era of a new day is advancing; the night is far spent; the day star is near. Man, the unit, contains the whole creation.

When man comes to the recognition of his kingship, he will exercise the leash of self-mastery, and gradually regain his lost inheritance. The product of his mind will recreate the earth. He will fight the dross of human experience inimical to progress, as plagues are now eradicated. The mind thus clarified will reflect signal beauty of countenance.

You ask about God. Think deeply; cherish the thought. Listen. Do you hear a voice in answer to the prayerful thought vibrating through the chamber of your interior self? Remember, O Soul, the within of you is open to the universal reservoir of the without! The nearness of God is incomparable—He is within you. "In Him I live and move and have my being." I need this divine essence. I breathe it. It is life; it is hope; it is sustaining; it is love.

I am only dead—a dead thing—when I fail to recognize my Lord, and I shrivel and starve in body and spirit. He is here in this Holy of Holies of my being, lighting the torch of fire which I wave out to the submerged humanities in this grief-stricken world.

Listen. Do you detect a lover's note vibrating in your empty heart, made desolate by war? Do you feel a thrill striking at your dead heart? Had you forgotten love—? You read this sacred page—your thought is stirred to action—you ponder the truth of my words from beyond the stars—you seek to know the Truth.

I claim that within the human personality there is proof of God and of immortality—we need only the lamp of God's love to shine into our hearts. Listen. Repeat the prayer you learned at mother's knee. The world carries about on its wounded breast, the babies' prayer.

Your lips are tired—you cannot frame the long-forgotten words—your soul is in agony of doubt—already the strength is there within you, waiting to meet your need. You feel the impulse of the Everlasting Arms beneath you; within is the Love of God.

CHAPTER XXVI
THE DRAMA OF WORLDS

NEW YORK CITY
March 19, 1917

Much interest is attached to this book, and a few desire to express briefly some sentiment in regard to Truth.

I have invited a few of my friends to participate in a discussion involving world movements at this time. In so doing we hope to prove first, individuality; and second, power to impress the subject matter in the mind of each individual present on the conscious, normal mind of our correspondent—inviting her to explain how she is able to differentiate speakers, how she is able to know various attitudes or gestures made by those who are only present in thought.

We have talked this event over and the consensus of opinion is that we assemble on the Westminster campus near the church. London is a favorite spot, for some of us are English by birth.

The gentlemen assembled here are: William Ewart Gladstone, William Shakespeare, Patrick Henry, Ralph Waldo Emerson, William Ellery Channing, Henry Ward Beecher, Disraeli, Abraham Lincoln, George Washington and William James.

The dictator of this paper has been elected chairman of the informal gathering, and invokes Divine

Aid in the success of the experiment which he hopes will add indubitable proof to the fact of life beyond. . . Turning to the assembled meeting, he speaks:

"Gentlemen, to me this is a solemn occasion. We are to be witnesses of a law until now untested by science. A pact made between two worlds, a combine of minds—ten minds assembled here under the shadow of Westminster in the tenuous atmosphere of space, against one mind on the other side of life, and dwelling on another continent."

William Gladstone moves to a space near the Chairman and extends his arms toward the sea while one hand is lifted as in reverent meditation:

"The event is unparalleled in the world's history. I observe a faint ray of light traversing the air as I think of the words I should utter on such occasion as this—my thoughts travel through space on this spiral air route, I notice that circles are described. There are no towers of observation, or visible means of converting or assembling thought waves. They circle as thin puffs of light, blown as thistledown. If words and intelligible sentences may be carried across the dark waters to America and record made of them in human conscious-ness, and legibly transcribed, then indeed may we un-derstand, for the God-made man stands fully revealed to the world."

"Here in my beloved England I wish to say, *Peace be unto thee; that righteous peace justified by right doing.*

To the Premier: 'As suddenly as war came—as suddenly it goes, leaving the fields white with the harvest for
the reaping.' "

The author and Mr. Gladstone turn and walk
toward the rear of the church, while a white-robed figure advances and I hear the name of William Shakespeare. Mr. Shakespeare does not commit his voice to
speech. He holds in one hand a branch—it looks like a
willow bough, the tiny green leaves tremble in the
breeze. He turns his face smiling toward America; he
studies the waters, lifts his face upward and watches the
flight of a seagull.

The Drama of Worlds imparts, an impetus to thought;
Time, winged with spears takes flight
Beneath the shadow of the night,
Strolling in heavy-hearted ease,
To see whate'er there be of light
Beyond this vale of tears,
In star-dimmed, fever-rimmed spheres.
Between the here and there, Methinks I see a gleam of
hope,
Rebound from wave crest sea of barren shore;
Further, O Sea, rebound and vibrant be
Thy never-ending rhapsody of glee;
Outstretch thy vibrant arm to mastery.
Methinks, mayhap 'twill trouble be,
When day comes lingering 'long
The path of all the yesterday
Of hope-strewn hours.

Oh, silence then
The songs that float untaught,
Give to the bird the song to sing
Of days that are to be,
Of nights agone; of flames erased;
Be gentle-minded; 'tis guard to thee within the fold;
Methinks the day enfolds the sphere above,
'Tis sight I get of rays beyond the dunes.
Get hither and begone, the sight of war
Interlude the space with plow and hoe.
Mingle thy shade with garlands green;
Betimes I see a beam of light
Stream bright above fair England's sky;
Avaunt, they darkened night, avaunt!

Lord Beaconsfield approaches within the enclosure. He pauses a moment to gather a flower. He sends a quick thought, inquiring if I can tell the name of the flower. I recognize a white chrysanthemum. He tells me that he wears this flower in honor of Japan; that Japan has taken her place before the nations of the world, established in equity and justice. My heart responds gratitude, while Lord Beaconsfield watches the approach of a German hydroplane which gradually rises and floats away in the sky. He speaks, watching the airplane, exclaiming:

"Intellect slain! Pity the people!"

Then, with upraised and smiling face, he extends his arms toward the English Channel and says:

The day-star approaches."

Then, as if to demonstrate the fact of immortality through the human personality, he inquires if I am able to read thoughts that are not directed to me. I respond by telling him that only as his thoughts mingle with mine through telepathic correspondence, am I able to know what he thinks about.

The author approaches and after a moment, informs me that they wish to speak separately of diametrically opposed matter in symposium, offering further test of conscious differentiation of personality.

Dr. James of Harvard suggests a point of cleavage. Henry Ward Beecher suggests the brain is a reflectograph, the process mental, spiritual, and highly psychic. William E. Charming wishes to know how far thought may travel without loss of energy.

Dr. James replies that it gains in power and energy, especially when unified with correlative thought.

George Washington observes that science is opening the walls of division between the two worlds—which the author demonstrates can be accomplished through the energizing power of knowledge applied when the human personality is generally understood by the world.

Mr. Lincoln wishes a private word with me and tells me that he knew my father and brother in the Civil War of 1860-1865. A thrill of pleasure and a smile of recognition at this—while Mr. Lincoln speaks of advancement of science and the understanding of spiritual laws. He commends the President of the United States:

"The President is wise in deferring war on Germany, for behind the warring element are the stricken people who are bearing heavy burdens imposed by autocracy. To war against the people would be ignominious; but to deprive the people of those who enslave and enthrall them, would be equity. This may only be accomplished by the people themselves who will throw off the yoke of bondage as Russia has done and as others in bondage will do. God haste the day of their deliverance!"

Patrick Henry extends to his beloved United States the warning of preparation.

"Be mindful of the past."

He declares the state of ease and wealth inimical to progress.

"Be stalwart, like men, girded and ready in body, firm in mind and by appointment, brave and gifted."

In military tactics, he advises special training of young people of both sexes.

NOTE BY THE CORRESPONDENT

The following incident may add further proof! Ralph Waldo Emerson was the last speaker to be introduced. So far, each one spoke distinctly and without hesitation, the message was recorded.

There seemed to be conveyed to my inner receptivity the scene enacted at London. I apprehended the movement of each speaker as related in this chapter.

Emerson was the last to speak. The world loves Emerson and I anticipated much from this interview, but, strange to relate, my pen refused to write. After waiting eagerly for some minutes, I gave up the work for the evening.

The next morning, I tried once and received just the few halting words—"I feel like a school boy."

The third morning I received the message from Mr. Emerson.

In commenting on this episode, a literary man in New York told the following story, saying, "That was characteristic of Emerson."

A number of Emerson's friends called one evening and during the visit, Emerson excused himself to write a telegram. After waiting a long while, his friends wondered at his prolonged delay.

They found him in his study pondering over the telegram. Glancing up with a look of perplexity on his face, he said:

"I cannot get this telegram in ten words."

CHAPTER XXVII
RALPH WALDO EMERSON

I am exceedingly desirous of improving the opportunity to add my quota to that which has already been said.

My philosophy has always been that of balance. Justice is the fulcrum of the individual soul by which each life must balance to maintain its equilibrium.

In the recognition of life as I have learned to define it, I observe the very complexity of it eludes minute inspection. It is through this avenue of research that we must now proceed if we would obtain proof of that which we seek to demonstrate. The balance of the soul—balance suggests equal distribution of whatsoever product weighed. The weight of responsibility adjusts itself to the wealth of the individual, whether that may consist of spiritual or material culture.

You will gather that whatever is sown will return in time—as seed tossed about by variable winds. Fortune gathers the same and returns the same in kind to the sower. It is compensation.

Analytical understanding of life is necessary to the student of life; without this understanding there is lack of balance. And those who refuse to gather wisdom from laws made for the enlightenment of the understanding, must remain on the plane of the untaught. To advance in wisdom is to throw aside the chains of conventionality. Ideas become fixed.

My student friend will at once realize that fixedness of ideas results in disuse of faculty and renders it impotent. The receptacle of thought becomes stagnated and when Truth is presented, the thought-waves are blunted, as a river in its advance to the sea becomes clogged with driftwood and debris.

Truth revealed elevates the consciousness; the light illumes the interior being. Ideas thus sharpened by contact with universal wisdom, gain strength by association and assimilation.

Faith is an attribute of soul product; it is used to balance values. Observe the chart, the old Book of Books, to ascertain for yourself how faith entered into the values of life experience. Everywhere the Book differentiates those who lived by faith and those who did not understand faith as a soul attribute.

To most people, the acceptance of faith, incomprehensible to understanding, will measure in the balance for knowledge. This is *persona grata;* the gift to the individual, the passport in lieu of coin.

Now abide these three: Faith, Hope and Love; but the greatest of these is Love. Faith comes first, as it opens the channels of receptivity to hope. Love enters and abides, where faith stands sentinel.

Imperial Host,
Within Thy tent of stars,
Guarded by Faith outside and Hope within,
Pity thine alien brother, Doubt, without.
Be swift.
Thy mantle bring, while angel voices sing
Hallelujahs to the King.

CHAPTER XXVIII
LETTER FROM THE AUTHOR

NEW YORK CITY
March 26, 1917

In reviewing the thought presented in these pages, I have endeavored to emphasize the human personality as the path to knowledge. If I have burdened the reader in my effort to explain Truth from my exalted standpoint, I have done so through my endeavor to explain Truth as it is, incorporate within the soul of man, which is often mistaken as without special value in relation to discovery.

My evidence is summed up with the essential premise, personality; if research still fails to substantiate evidence, then must the cycle of time engage in still further revolutions through space until time and culture of faculty obtains discernment.

I have given to the world lighted by the torch of fire, a light that shines unto the perfect day. It is mine to spread this fire abroad, gifted with Divine understanding, granted to opportunity through individual culture. It is my privilege to employ my God-given power in spreading this light to those who sit in darkness and suffer in the chains of war and desolation. I spread the light. God never leaves nor forsakes His people. When the emergency comes, God also comes to meet common need. Man's importunity is God's opportunity. He is the Father of mankind. This is Truth. The essential need of the world is recognition of this fact. We are born of Him—one with Him. He suffers with us, meets our need. Not to recognize this truth is to fail in our study of the personality.

"I am come that ye might have life more abundant."

We have not yet reached the experience of abundant Life until we emerge from our chrysalis of ignorance into the development of understanding, awaiting culture through Christ.

The beautiful plan of creation unfolds to the understanding of the developed soul made perfect as Christ is perfect; having within itself the culture of creation, the heritage of kingship, that oneness with the Divine, and the mastery of the world.

Faithfully yours,
(Signed) FREDERIC W. H. MYERS

AFTERWORD

GRACE (DUFFIE BOYLAN) GELDERT
National President, League of American Penwomen
October 1, 1923

Here is a book which answers humanity's persistent questions: "What is that which is over the hills? What is beyond the lost horizon? Where is the flame from the blown out lamp?"

Beaten by doubt, driven by anguish, the race has been forever lifting that one wild cry. But although men and angels have ever made answer, the world has been slow to see and hear and understand that the soul is an immortal thing and that there is no death.

Juliet S. Goodenow has transcribed the extraordinary correspondence between herself and a distinguished scientist, who was foremost among the psychics of his day on earth, and who is now carrying on his tremendous purpose to coordinate the work of the visible and the invisible spheres from his point of vantage in the heavens.

Mrs. Goodenow is not a member of any spiritualistic cult. She knows nothing of mediums or methods of communication with those who are unseen, save only this: She has been addressed, as was one other, by the angel who said: "I say unto thee: WRITE." And she has written what she has been given to proclaim to the world the proofs of IMMORTALITY.

ABOUT JULIET GOODENOW

Juliet Sophia Duffie Goodenow was born in Kalama-zoo, Michigan in 1853, one of eleven children of Phelix K. and Juliette Duffie. Her father, who emigrated from Ireland, owned the Dollar House Hotel in Kalamazoo. During the American Civil War he served for eighteen months as a Captain in the 19th Michigan Infantry, Company K, and her brother Malcolm served as a private and drummer in the same company.

In 1878, on New Year's Day, Juliet Sophia Duffie married George Irish Goodenow, a wireless telegrapher and traveling salesman. They had three children.

Mrs. Goodenow was very active in the Kalamazoo, Michigan community: in 1892 she was President of the Twentieth Century Club; in 1903 she initiated a petition signed by 27 women to encourage the Michigan House of Representatives to pass a pending bill which would allow women to be appointed as members of certain state boards. In 1906, as chair of the Industrial Committee of the Michigan State Federation of Women's Clubs, she initiated a petition to the Michigan Senate, on behalf of all of Michigan's women's clubs, recommending the enforcement of child labor laws, particularly in Michigan factories and also for paperboys who were often out delivering afternoon newspapers past midnight.

Juliet Goodenow died in Michigan in 1926.

Printed in Great Britain
by Amazon

25086083R00086